# STATES OF WONDER

*Puzzles for Learning State Facts*

# STATES OF WONDER

*Puzzles for Learning State Facts*

*Jeanne Cheyney*
*Arnold Cheyney*

**Good Year Books**

*Parsippany, New Jersey*

*To Jason and Vanessa Cheyney for their valuable help in the preparation of this manuscript.*

**Good Year Books**
are available for preschool through grade 6 for every basic curriculum subject plus many enrichment areas. For more Good Year Books, contact your local bookseller or educational dealer. For a complete catalog with information about other Good Year Books, please write:

**Good Year Books**
An imprint of Pearson Learning
299 Jefferson Road
Parsippany, New Jersey 07054-0480
1-800-321-3106
www.pearsonlearning.com

ISBN 0-673-46352-4

11 12 13 MAL 03 02

The United States is a great place to live and a wonderful place to experience. Those of us who travel abroad are always glad to return to its shores. We created *States of Wonder* so that students can develop a better understanding of our marvelous country.

For every state, we have included a crossword puzzle and additional games. We have tried to help students recognize interrelationships among states through these games and activities. Maps, encyclopedias, and social studies texts will help students determine the answers. Children can work in groups of two or three, or word games can be used as homework.

Upon request, the tourist-information agencies listed in this book will provide more information about their states.

Make copies of the blank grid so students can develop their own word games.

The content for *States of Wonder* was compiled from the World Book Encyclopedia, state travel brochures, and other reference sources. Even so, change is so rapid in our country that, soon after this book is in print, changing leadership in agriculture or industry may occur. But change provides an opportunity to point out the dynamic nature of our democracy, leaving us always with a sense of surprise and wonder.

Jeanne Cheyney
Arnold Cheyney

# CONTENTS

# STATE
# PUZZLES

# ALABAMA

NAME _____  DATE _____

25. Most valuable crop
26. Northern border state (abbr.)
27. A field crop: _____ crop
28. State abbr.
29. Eastern border river

## DOWN
1. Major seaport
2. Most valuable farm product
5. Southern border body of water: Gulf of _____
7. Wild flower species
8. Insect enemy of cotton
9. Important fruit crop
10. Famous black educator: Booker T. _____
12. Southern border state (abbr.)
13. Civil rights leader: M. L. _____, Jr.
16. Western border state (abbr.)
18. A crop
19. A field crop
21. Valuable farm animals
22. Important fruit crop
23. A river

## ALABAMA CROSSWORD PUZZLE

### ACROSS
1. Capital city
3. Famous deaf and blind woman: Helen _____
4. Largest city
6. Important nut crop
11. Famous scientist: George Washington _____
14. Alabama is called "The Heart of _____."
15. Confederate president: Jefferson _____
17. State tree: Southern _____
20. A poultry product
24. A lake and stream fish

*boll weevil*

From *States of Wonder* published by GoodYearBooks. Copyright © 1992 Jeanne Cheyney and Arnold Cheyney.

# ALABAMA

NAME _____ DATE _____

## ALABAMA WORD SEARCHING

### DIRECTIONS

Find these hidden Alabama words in the grid (the words not in parentheses). They can go up, down, across, at an angle, forward, or backward.

Rivers:
  Alabama
  (Black) Warrior
  Coosa
  Tallapoosa
  Tombigbee (longest river)
trolley (first electric, 1866)
bayou (shallow, slow water)
Cities:
  Mobile
  Dothan
  Montgomery
  Birmingham
  Tuscaloosa
  Gadsden
  Huntsville
Sequoyah (beautiful cavern)
forests (cover two-thirds of AL)
alligators (swamp)
(Southern) Pine (state tree)
Coastal fishing catch:
  crab
  oyster
  shrimp

| M | C | H | B | D | T | J | L | E | Y | S | F | I |
|---|---|---|---|---|---|---|---|---|---|---|---|---|
| O | N | T | A | P | U | T | G | O | A | T | S | M |
| N | B | R | Y | D | S | O | C | O | O | S | A | G |
| T | H | T | O | V | C | M | A | W | S | E | C | A |
| G | U | Q | U | D | A | B | H | W | M | R | B | D |
| O | N | S | A | L | L | I | G | A | T | O | R | S |
| M | T | C | G | T | O | G | U | R | I | F | N | D |
| E | S | A | Y | R | O | B | A | R | L | M | A | E |
| R | V | O | L | O | S | E | T | I | U | H | L | N |
| Y | I | S | S | L | A | E | D | O | T | H | A | N |
| C | L | E | U | L | A | H | R | R | D | V | B | F |
| W | L | Q | B | E | C | P | G | E | K | R | A | Q |
| B | E | U | P | Y | E | M | O | P | T | E | M | Y |
| E | M | O | B | I | L | E | L | O | R | S | A | F |
| N | T | Y | C | R | A | B | N | T | S | D | Y | E |
| I | K | A | P | S | H | R | I | M | P | A | C | O |
| P | Q | H | M | A | H | G | N | I | M | R | I | B |

*Helen Keller*

From *States of Wonder* published by GoodYearBooks. Copyright © 1992 Jeanne Cheyney and Arnold Cheyney.

3

# ALASKA

NAME _____     DATE _____

20. The Haida _____ tribe carved totem poles.
24. Asian country nearest Alaska
28. City with largest population
29. Largest and chief river

## DOWN
2. Pribilof Island: world's largest herd of _____ (fur animal)
4. Alaska is the _____ U.S. state.
6. Rivers of ice
8. Eastern border country
14. State tree: Sitka _____
15. Aleutian Island farthest from mainland
17. Eskimos keep _____ for meat and hides.
19. Nome is located on the _____ Sound.
21. Town farthest north
22. Most valuable livestock product
23. Important fish
25. Body of water west of AK: Bering _____
26. Aleutian Island and naval station
27. The oil pipeline begins at Prudhoe _____.

## ALASKA CROSSWORD PUZZLE

### ACROSS
1. Has many active _____
3. Most valuable mineral
5. Oil port
6. Discovered in 1898
7. Highest U.S. peak: Mt. _____
9. State abbr.
10. A Pribilof Island: St. _____
11. Capital city
12. _____ were once traded with Russia.
13. Northern border ocean
16. State bird: Willow _____
18. Natives of Alaska

4

*sitka spruce*

From States of Wonder published by GoodYearBooks. Copyright © 1992 Jeanne Cheney and Arnold Cheyney.

NAME _____ DATE _____

## ALASKA PAIRS OF ISLAND NAMES

### DIRECTIONS

All of the island names in the rectangle are written twice, except for one. Write the name of each island pair on a blank. (Cross off the pairs as you find them.) Then find the name of the island that appears only once and write it in the box.

_____

_____

_____

_____

_____

_____

_____

ADAK AMLIA ST. GEORGE UNIMAK FOUR MOUNTAINS
FOX KISKA ATTU SANAK AMLIA TRINITY ST. GEORGE ST. MATTHEW MONTAGUE
AGATTU AMICHITKA MIDDLETON NUNIVAK MONTAGUE TRINITY FOX CHIRIKOF TANAGA
TRINITY CHIRIKOF RAT SANAK ST. MATTHEW ST. GEORGE AGATTU ST. PAUL
ANDREANOF ATTU UNIMAK KODIAK NUNIVAK TANAGA ST. PAUL ST. LAWRENCE RAT ADAK KISKA
FOUR MOUNTAINS ANDREANOF ST. LAWRENCE AMICHITKA MIDDLETON

_____

_____

_____

_____

_____

_____

_____

_____   _____

_____   _____   _____

_____   _____   _____

[   ]

## ALASKA NAME THE CITY

### DIRECTIONS

Fill in the dotted lines with your answers. If they are correct, the circled letters will spell a city's name.

1. Timber is an important _____ product.   1.

2. World's largest gathering of Bald _____: along the Chilkat River   2.

3. "Marine Highway": Alaska's _____ system   3.

4. Sea southwest of Alaska   4.

5. Large, fierce wild animal   5.

6. Name of the string of Alaskan Islands   6.

7. Farmers raise _____.   7.

8. Most valuable livestock product   8.

9. U.S. Secretary of State William H. _____ bought Alaska in 1867.   9.

totem pole

eagle

5

# ARIZONA

NAME _____   DATE _____

25. A western border state (abbr.)
26. State abbr.
28. Desert summers are _____.
29. Farmers _____ their land.
30. State flower: _____ (Saguaro) cactus
31. Poisonous lizard: _____ monster
32. A plant: organ-_____ cactus
33. Important farm animal

## DOWN
1. Southeast border country
2. Famous western boomtown
3. A mountain stream waterfall: Bridal _____
4. A huge crater
8. Dams generate _____ power.
10. Capital city
12. Tourists visit the _____ Desert.
15. September: Navajo Tribal _____
16. Tuscon: world's _____ capital
18. A dam: _____ Canyon
20. A lake
21. A dam
23. Important farm animals
24. A western border state (abbr.)
27. Arizona mountains: largest U.S. Ponderosa _____ area

## ARIZONA CROSSWORD PUZZLE

### ACROSS
1. _____ and plateaus cover half of Arizona.
5. Valuable mined mineral
6. U.S. government built _____ to hold water.
7. A leading producer of citrus _____
9. Conquerors from _____ once ruled Arizona.
11. A field crop
13. Important crop
14. An eastern border state (abbr.)
17. An eastern border state (abbr.)
19. 153,000 _____ live in Arizona.
22. Called "The Grand _____ State"

6

From *States of Wonder* published by GoodYearBooks. Copyright © 1992 Jeanne Cheyney and Arnold Cheyney.

# ARIZONA

NAME _____

DATE _____

## ARIZONA CROSSING OVER

### DIRECTIONS

Use a pencil for this game. Find words from the following list that have the correct number of spaces and letters to fit into the crossing-over boxes (the words not in parentheses). Each word has a place where it belongs. The first word is done for you. To continue, find a 7-letter word with "g" in the fourth space, and so on. All the words tell about Arizona.

**3 letters**
Ajo (town)
San (Saint)
dam (water and power)
hay

**4 letters**
deer
wren (state bird)
pine
Hopi (Indians)
Gila (river)
Salt (river)
Pima (Indians)
corn
Dome (Rock Mts.)

**5 letters**
sheep
wheat
Black (Mts.)
Grand (Canyon)
Table (Mt.)
fruit (citrus)
grain

**6 letters**
Mojave (Desert)
cactus (plant)
Navajo (Indians)
Mohawk (Mts.)
cattle
Tucson (city)
desert
Hoover (Dam)
Marble (Canyon)
silver (mined)
cotton

**7 letters**
Phoenix (capital)

Painted (Desert)
Cochise (Indian chief)
lettuce
sorghum (grain)

**8 letters**
Geronimo (warrior)
Colorado (river)
Bartlett (Dam)
Hualapai (Indians)
Cimarron (Mts.)
Coolidge (Dam)

**9 letters**
Tombstone (historic town)
Flagstaff (city)
petroleum
gemstones (mined)
Horseshoe (Reservoir)
Roosevelt (Dam)
Petrified (Forest)

F L A G S T A F F

*Saguaro cactus*

*Indian*

7

NAME _____

DATE _____

26. A U.S. leader in growing _____
28. Lake and river fish
29. Produces about a third of U.S. _____ crop
30. _____ once owned Arkansas.
31. State flower: _____ blossom
32. A common bird
33. Turkeys: an important _____ product
34. State beverage
35. Leading state in raising young chickens called _____

## DOWN
1. A river
2. A mountain range
3. Arkansas was discovered by _____.
4. State abbr.
5. Northern border state (abbr.)
6. Amusement park: _____ Patch, USA
9. The largest _____ hatchery in U.S.
10. Leading forest product
13. Southern border state (abbr.)
15. A tree
16. Farm animals
17. State insect: _____ bee
18. Eastern border river
21. Western border state (abbr.)
23. A field crop
24. Largest river within the state
25. Important farm animal: _____ cattle
27. _____ once owned Arkansas

## ARKANSAS CROSSWORD PUZZLE

### ACROSS
1. Capital city: Little _____
3. The only active _____ mine in U.S.
7. State tree: _____
8. Important poultry product
11. Important supply base for travelers (1817): _____ Smith
12. World-famous health center: _____ Springs
14. One of the largest springs in the U.S.: _____ Springs
19. Important field crop
20. A creek
22. Lake and river fish
25. A river

# ARKANSAS

NAME _____    DATE _____

## ARKANSAS NUMBER CODE

### DIRECTIONS

Look at the numbers under each line. Find the matching numbers in the code box and write the letters on the corresponding answer lines.

|  |
|------|
| A – 1 |
| B – 2 |
| C – 3 |
| D – 4 |
| E – 5 |
| F – 6 |
| G – 7 |
| H – 8 |
| I – 9 |
| J – 10 |
| K – 11 |
| L – 12 |
| M – 13 |
| N – 14 |
| O – 15 |
| P – 16 |
| Q – 17 |
| R – 18 |
| S – 19 |
| T – 20 |
| U – 21 |
| V – 22 |
| W – 23 |
| X – 24 |
| Y – 25 |
| Z – 26 |

1. Arkansas has something that no other U.S. state has. What is it?

$\overline{3}\ \overline{18}\ \overline{1}\ \overline{20}\ \overline{5}\ \overline{18}$   $\overline{15}\ \overline{6}$   $\overline{4}\ \overline{9}\ \overline{1}\ \overline{13}\ \overline{15}\ \overline{14}\ \overline{4}\ \overline{19}$   $\overline{19}\ \overline{20}\ \overline{1}\ \overline{20}\ \overline{5}$

$\overline{16}\ \overline{1}\ \overline{18}\ \overline{11}$ :   $\overline{1}\ \overline{14}$   $\overline{1}\ \overline{3}\ \overline{20}\ \overline{9}\ \overline{22}\ \overline{5}$   $\overline{4}\ \overline{9}\ \overline{1}\ \overline{13}\ \overline{15}\ \overline{14}\ \overline{4}$

$\overline{13}\ \overline{9}\ \overline{14}\ \overline{5}$   $\overline{14}\ \overline{5}\ \overline{1}\ \overline{18}$   $\overline{13}\ \overline{21}\ \overline{18}\ \overline{6}\ \overline{18}\ \overline{5}\ \overline{5}\ \overline{19}\ \overline{2}\ \overline{15}\ \overline{18}\ \overline{15}$ .

$\overline{20}\ \overline{15}\ \overline{21}\ \overline{18}\ \overline{9}\ \overline{19}\ \overline{20}\ \overline{19}$   $\overline{23}\ \overline{8}\ \overline{15}$   $\overline{6}\ \overline{9}\ \overline{14}\ \overline{4}$   $\overline{4}\ \overline{9}\ \overline{1}\ \overline{13}\ \overline{15}\ \overline{14}\ \overline{4}\ \overline{19}$

$\overline{20}\ \overline{8}\ \overline{5}\ \overline{18}\ \overline{5}$   $\overline{13}\ \overline{1}\ \overline{25}$   $\overline{11}\ \overline{5}\ \overline{5}\ \overline{16}$   $\overline{20}\ \overline{8}\ \overline{5}\ \overline{13}$ .

2. Arkansas has something else that no other state has. What is it?

$\overline{20}\ \overline{8}\ \overline{5}$   $\overline{12}\ \overline{1}\ \overline{18}\ \overline{7}\ \overline{5}\ \overline{19}\ \overline{20}$   $\overline{7}\ \overline{15}\ \overline{22}\ \overline{5}\ \overline{18}\ \overline{14}\ \overline{13}\ \overline{5}\ \overline{14}\ \overline{20}$

$\overline{20}\ \overline{18}\ \overline{15}\ \overline{21}\ \overline{20}$   $\overline{8}\ \overline{1}\ \overline{20}\ \overline{3}\ \overline{8}\ \overline{5}\ \overline{18}\ \overline{25}$   $\overline{9}\ \overline{14}$   $\overline{20}\ \overline{8}\ \overline{5}$   $\overline{21}\ \overline{19}$

3. Three main Indian tribes lived in Arkansas. What were their names?

$\overline{3}\ \overline{1}\ \overline{4}\ \overline{4}\ \overline{15}$   $\overline{15}\ \overline{19}\ \overline{1}\ \overline{7}\ \overline{5}$   $\overline{17}\ \overline{21}\ \overline{1}\ \overline{16}\ \overline{1}\ \overline{23}$

4. Who crossed Arkansas in about 1541?

$\overline{8}\ \overline{5}\ \overline{18}\ \overline{14}\ \overline{1}\ \overline{14}\ \overline{4}\ \overline{15}$   $\overline{4}\ \overline{5}$   $\overline{19}\ \overline{15}\ \overline{20}\ \overline{15}$ '   $\overline{1}$   $\overline{19}\ \overline{16}\ \overline{1}\ \overline{14}\ \overline{9}\ \overline{19}\ \overline{8}$

$\overline{5}\ \overline{24}\ \overline{16}\ \overline{12}\ \overline{15}\ \overline{18}\ \overline{5}\ \overline{18}$ '   $\overline{3}\ \overline{18}\ \overline{15}\ \overline{19}\ \overline{19}\ \overline{5}\ \overline{4}$   $\overline{20}\ \overline{8}\ \overline{5}$

$\overline{13}\ \overline{9}\ \overline{19}\ \overline{19}\ \overline{9}\ \overline{19}\ \overline{19}\ \overline{9}\ \overline{16}\ \overline{16}\ \overline{9}$   $\overline{18}$ .   $\overline{1}\ \overline{14}\ \overline{4}$   $\overline{23}\ \overline{5}\ \overline{14}\ \overline{20}$

$\overline{1}\ \overline{3}\ \overline{18}\ \overline{15}\ \overline{19}\ \overline{19}$   $\overline{1}\ \overline{18}\ \overline{11}\ \overline{1}\ \overline{14}\ \overline{19}\ \overline{1}\ \overline{19}$   $\overline{20}\ \overline{15}$   $\overline{20}\ \overline{8}\ \overline{5}$

$\overline{15}\ \overline{26}\ \overline{1}\ \overline{18}\ \overline{11}\ \overline{19}$ .

5. What river cuts across Arkansas?

$\overline{1}\ \overline{18}\ \overline{11}\ \overline{1}\ \overline{14}\ \overline{19}\ \overline{1}\ \overline{19}$   $\overline{18}\ \overline{9}\ \overline{22}\ \overline{5}\ \overline{18}$

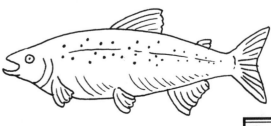

*trout*

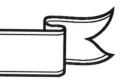

# CALIFORNIA

NAME _____    DATE _____

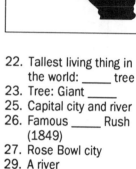

22. Tallest living thing in the world: _____ tree
23. Tree: Giant _____
25. Capital city and river
26. Famous _____ Rush (1849)
27. Rose Bowl city
29. A river
30. Important farm animals

**DOWN**
1. State flower: Golden _____
2. State abbr.
3. A break in the earth's crust: St. Andreas _____
4. A large city: San _____
6. Center of the state is _____ land
8. A common hardwood tree
11. Most valuable ocean fish
12. Famous southern factories produce air _____
13. Important fruit crop
14. Tournament of _____ (January 1st)
15. Movie industry location
16. Naturalist and founder of Sierra Club
21. Famous amusement park: _____ land
24. Southern border country
26. One of the world's longest suspension bridges: Golden _____
28. An eastern border state (abbr.)

## CALIFORNIA CROSSWORD PUZZLE

**ACROSS**
1. Western border ocean
5. Northern border state (abbr.)
7. California has more _____ than any other state.
9. Sudden earth movement: earth_____
10. Famous berry farm
13. California is called "The _____ State."
17. High mountain range near eastern border: Sierra _____
18. Famous animal home: San Diego _____
19. An eastern border state (abbr.)
20. Barren desert wasteland: _____ Desert

10

From *States of Wonder* published by GoodYearBooks. Copyright © 1992 Jeanne Cheyney and Arnold Cheyney.

# CALIFORNIA

NAME _____ DATE _____

## CALIFORNIA NAME THE CITY

### DIRECTIONS
Fill in the dotted lines with your answers. If they are correct, the circled letters will spell the name of a California city.

1. Largest city
2. A long river
3. City with first cable car
4. Farmers raise fine ____.
5. A citrus fruit
6. A national park
7. Most valuable farm animal
8. Famous amusement park
9. Lowest point in U.S. having the highest recorded temperature
10. Famous bay bridge

## CALIFORNIA SCRAMBLED MOUNTAINS

### DIRECTIONS
Unscramble the words and write the answers on the lines provided. (Use scrap paper to work out your answers.)

1. R D E

2. A E H C C O O L T

3. A L N O S M

4. N S A   N R E A B N D I R O

5. A N S   E A F R A L

6. T A S N A   R C Z U

7. R I R S E A   A E A N V D

8. A I Z F E R R

## CALIFORNIA WORDS IN WORDS

How many words can you make from the letters in "Fantasy Castle," a building at Disneyland?

### FANTASY CASTLE

1. _____
2. _____
3. _____
4. _____

5. _____
6. _____
7. _____
8. _____

9. _____
10. _____
11. _____
12. _____

13. _____
14. _____

11

NAME _____ DATE _____

29. Important field crop
32. Important vegetable crop
33. Western border state (abbr.)
34. Large wild animal
35. Colorado mines gold and _____.
36. Important liquid mineral

**DOWN**

2. Denver: known as the _____ to the Rockies
3. Large wild animal
4. Most important field crop
5. Called "The _____ State"
8. Aspen: largest silver _____ ever found in North America (1894)
11. State tree: Blue _____
12. Prickly, dry-area plant
14. Important field crop
16. Capital and largest city
17. One of the most valuable animal products
19. State abbr.
20. A southern border state (abbr.)
21. A southern border state (abbr.)
22. A northern border state (abbr.)
23. U.S. government owns over one-_____ of CO
26. Lookout Mt.: grave of _____ Bill
27. A dry-area plant: _____brush
28. Valuable farm and ranch animals
30. National park: Mesa _____
31. The U.S. _____ in Denver makes coins.

## COLORADO CROSSWORD PUZZLE

**ACROSS**

1. World's highest suspension bridge is over Royal _____.
6. Eastern border state (abbr.)
7. World-famous ski resort
9. Important field crop: sugar _____
10. Probably the most important and famous Rocky Mt. peak: _____ Peak
13. An Indian reservation
15. Near Colorado Springs: U.S. Air Force _____
18. Western mountain range
24. Northern border state (abbr.)
25. Colorado is the Spanish word for "colored _____."
27. A leading producer of _____ (animal)

From *States of Wonder* published by GoodYearBooks. Copyright © 1992 Jeanne Cheyney and Arnold Cheyney.

NAME _____     DATE _____

## COLORADO SUPPLY THE VOWEL

### DIRECTIONS

Look for the following words in the grid (the words not in parentheses). The words can go up, down, across, at angles, backward, or forward. Parts of words may overlap. Supply the correct vowel—*a e i o u*—for the center of each word group.

corn
Kiowa (Indians)
hay
(Great Sand) Dunes
    (National Monument)
Rocky (Mts.)
(Fort) Collins (city)
Estes (Park, a city)
(South) Platte (river)
yucca (plant)
Cheyenne (Indians)
cottonwood (tree)
Pawnee (Indians)
Boulder (city)
elk (largest U.S. herd)
Pueblo (city)
nuclear (power plants)
chinook (warm winter wind
    blowing down eastern
    slopes)
onion (crop)
(Royal) Gorge (Canyon)

| P | A | L | D | U | F | Q | S | E | T | W | Q | B |
|---|---|---|---|---|---|---|---|---|---|---|---|---|
| I | L | R | Y | C | W | L | H | F | G | O | K | M |
| Y | P | ○ | W | N | E | E | R | E | S | R | C | C |
| T | H | E | T | O | N | C | S | Y | K | C | ○ | R |
| E | I | L | F | T | F | T | G | D | J | R | T | G |
| G | E | C | C | H | ○ | Y | E | N | N | E | T | O |
| M | S | U | K | S | L | P | D | E | R | B | O | Z |
| P | K | N | Q | U | K | A | V | W | J | T | N | R |
| S | E | C | J | N | Q | V | H | C | A | N | W | F |
| V | N | K | O | P | B | M | W | Y | R | D | O | B |
| C | H | ○ | N | O | O | K | L | G | E | I | O | N |
| U | N | O | L | H | B | I | O | I | D | K | D | P |
| O | M | W | S | L | R | D | Q | D | L | Y | E | H |
| C | P | A | X | T | O | L | B | E | ○ | P | O | J |
| A | Y | L | J | N | W | C | V | C | O | N | U | G |
| D | G | C | Y | K | F | M | C | H | B | I | E | A |
| L | N | A | Z | H | K | A | B | Y | E | M | G | S |

*skiing*

13

# CONNECTICUT

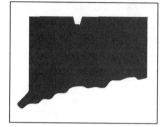

22. Hartford is known as the "_____ city."
24. Samuel _____ invented the repeating pistol.
25. Important dairy product
26. A vegetable crop
27. A Revolutionary War traitor: Benedict _____
29. Nautilus: world's first nuclear-powered _____ (abbr.)
30. State bird

**DOWN**

1. Valuable poultry product
3. Produces _____ aircraft engines
4. Block, a _____ explorer, claimed CT for his country.
5. Early powerful Indian tribe
7. Western border state (abbr.)
10. The earliest colonists were _____.
11. Hartford County: first _____ manufacturing
12. Called "The _____ State"
14. Connecticut: where Americans first made rubber _____
16. First insurance _____ sold (1864)
19. Pattison brothers were the first door-to-door _____.
20. Important fishing catch
23. _____ Whitney: famous inventor
28. Eastern border state (abbr.)

## CONNECTICUT CROSSWORD PUZZLE

**ACROSS**

1. First permanent colonists
2. Northern border state (abbr.)
6. In small towns, a _____ is a public park.
8. Many people _____ to work in New York City.
9. State abbr.
12. Important crop
13. Capital city
15. State's outlet to the ocean: Long Island _____
17. Chief field crop
18. Important fruit crop
21. Connecticut: the _____ smallest state

From *States of Wonder* published by GoodYearBooks. Copyright © 1992 Jeanne Cheyney and Arnold Cheyney.

# CONNECTICUT

NAME _____ DATE _____

## CONNECTICUT MORSE CODE

### DIRECTIONS

Look at the dots and dashes under each line. Find the matching dots and dashes in the code box and write the code letters on the answer lines.

| | |
|---|---|
| A | . _ |
| B | _ . . . |
| C | _ . _ . |
| D | _ . . |
| E | . |
| F | . . _ . |
| G | _ _ . |
| H | . . . . |
| I | . . |
| J | . _ _ _ |
| K | _ . _ |
| L | . _ . . |
| M | _ _ |
| N | _ . |
| O | _ _ _ |
| P | . _ _ . |
| Q | _ _ . _ |
| R | . _ . |
| S | . . . |
| T | _ |
| U | . . _ |
| V | . . . _ |
| W | . _ _ |
| X | _ . . _ |
| Y | _ . _ _ |
| Z | _ _ . . |

1. What was published in 1796?

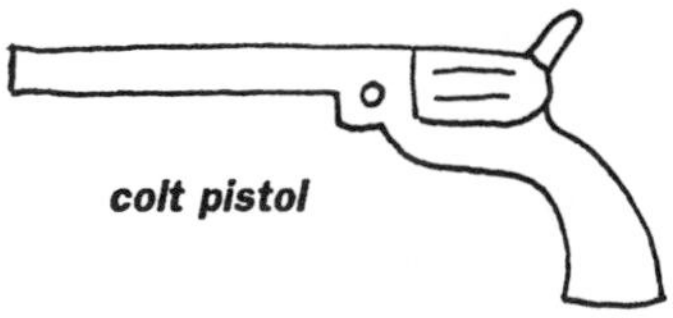

colt pistol

2. What is a famous historic seaport? What does it have?

tobacco

3. What is the largest lake? Why was it made?

4. What river cuts across the center of the state?

15

# DELAWARE

NAME _____ DATE _____

26. A Confederate
    stronghold: _____
    Delaware
27. Most of Delaware is
    _____.
28. Coastal fishing catch
29. Important greenhouse
    crop

**DOWN**
1. Largest river
2. English explorer _____
   sailed up the Delaware
   in 1609.
3. Northern border state
   (abbr.)
9. A vegetable crop
11. _____: sometimes
    called the chemical
    capital of the world
15. Valuable poultry
    product
17. Forests cover about
    one-_____ of Delaware.
18. State abbr.
21. Lake and river fish
22. A vegetable crop
23. State tree: American
    _____
24. A fruit crop
26. A wild animal

## DELAWARE CROSSWORD PUZZLE

**ACROSS**
1. A large chemical
   company
4. A leading poultry
   product
5. Lake and stream fish
6. Southeast border
   ocean
7. Southwest border state
   (abbr.)
8. Fruit crop
10. A field crop
12. An Indian tribe
13. A leading poultry animal
14. A farm product
16. A vegetable
19. State bird: Blue hen
20. Livestock animals
21. Valuable field crop
25. Capital city

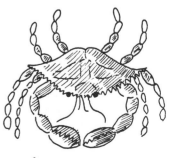

*crab*

From *States of Wonder* published by GoodYearBooks. Copyright © 1992 Jeanne Cheyney and Arnold Cheyney.

# DELAWARE

NAME _____ DATE _____

## DELAWARE CROSSING OVER

### DIRECTIONS
Use a pencil for this game. Find words from the following list that have the correct number of spaces and letters to fit into the crossing-over boxes (the words not in parentheses). Each word has a place where it belongs. The first word is done for you. To continue, find a ten-letter word with an "a" in the fifth space, and so on. All the words tell about Delaware.

3 letters
  eel (fish)
  fox
  oak
  pea
4 letters
  pine
  hogs
  corn
  carp (fish)
  eggs
  deer
  bass (fish)
  beef
  milk
  shad (fish)
  Port (Penny: a small town)
  Star (Hill: a small town)
5 letters
  beans
  crabs
  perch (fish)
  otter (animal)
  wheat
  trout (fish)
  clams
  Dutch (once owned DE)
  nylon (developed)
  paper (products manufac-
      tured)
  (State) house (old capitol)
  Dover (capital)
6 letters
  barley
  tupelo (tree)
  cherry
  tomato
  willow (tree)
  rabbit
  apples
  duPont (chemical
      manufacturer)
  Smyrna (river)
  Porter (small town)

7 letters
  oysters
  catfish
  hickory
  muskrat
  cypress (tree)
  turtles
  turkeys
8 letters
  soybeans
  broilers (young chickens)
  cucumber
  magnolia (tree)

  sweetgum (tree)
9 letters
  mushrooms
  sassafras (tree)
  Greenwood (small town)
10 letters
  cantaloupe
  watermelon
11 letters
  blueberries
  cranberries

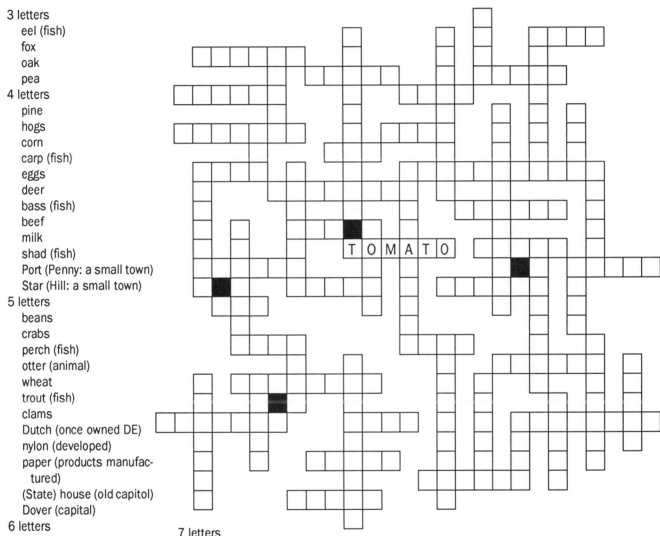

TOMATO

*sea turtle*

17

NAME _____ DATE _____

20. Indian tribe
27. Florida is a long _____.
28. Important dairy product
30. Important farm
    animals: _____ cattle
31. Famous amusement
    area: _____World

## DOWN
1. Poultry product
2. Northern border state
   (abbr.)
3. _____ shuttles are
   launched at Cape
   Canaveral.
4. Winter resort city
7. Severe storm
8. String of southern
   islands: Florida _____
11. Coastal water catch
13. Many _____ come to
    Florida.
18. A citrus fruit
20. Important Key West
    fishing catch
21. Important citrus crop
22. A southernmost U. S.
    city: Key _____
23. A farm crop
24. Western border body of
    water: _____ of Mexico
25. Important field crop:
    sugar _____
26. Large Panhandle town:
    Panama _____
29. State abbr.

## FLORIDA CROSSWORD PUZZLE

### ACROSS
1. National park at
   southern tip
5. An east-coast city: Palm
   _____
6. Florida: once owned by
   _____
9. A northern border state
   (abbr.)
10. Called "The _____
    State"
12. State park: Pennekamp
    Coral _____
14. A west-coast city: Ft.
    _____
15. Oranges are a _____
    fruit.
16. Everglades and swamp
    animal
17. State tree: Sabal _____
19. A citrus fruit: _____fruit

oranges

From *States of Wonder* published by GoodYearBooks. Copyright © 1992 Jeanne Cheyney and Arnold Cheyney.

# F L O R I D A

NAME _____   DATE _____

## FLORIDA NAME THE CITY

### DIRECTIONS
Fill in the dotted lines with your answers. If they are correct, the circled letters will spell the name of a Florida city.

1. Oldest U.S. city
2. Largest city
3. First federal wildlife refuge
4. Home of University of Miami football team
5. Most important winter vegetable crop
6. A river
7. Eastern border body of water
8. A popular South Florida Christmas flower
9. Largest of the Florida springs
10. Largest lake in the southern U.S.
11. A graceful white bird that eats cattle pests

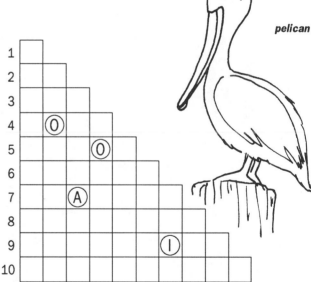

*pelican*

## FLORIDA SKYSCRAPER

### DIRECTIONS
Write your answers in the boxes. The circled letters will help you.

1. Abbr. for lake
2. Florida abbr.
3. Coastal water fish: _____ snapper
4. North Florida vegetable crop
5. North Florida fruit crop
6. Panhandle city: _____ City
7. North Florida food crop
8. Everglades Indian tribe
9. Citrus fruit
10. A west Florida city: St. _____

## FLORIDA WORDS IN WORDS

How many words can you make from the letters in "Peninsula State," which Florida is sometimes called because it extends 400 miles into the sea?

### PENINSULA STATE

1. _____
2. _____
3. _____
4. _____
5. _____
6. _____
7. _____
8. _____
9. _____
10. _____
11. _____
12. _____
13. _____
14. _____

19

NAME _____    DATE _____

30. Large city
32. Coastal water catch
34. Large city

**DOWN**
2. Birthplace of 39th U. S. President: Jimmy Carter
3. Important crop
4. Large city
5. Capital city
6. A northern border state (abbr.)
7. River catch: cat____
9. Important nut crop
10. Eastern border state (abbr.)
15. Farm animals
16. A northern border state (abbr.)
17. Famous song writer: Steven ____
18. Farm animals: ____ cattle
21. Famous river
23. Large city
28. Lake and river fish
29. Eli Whitney invented the cotton ____
31. Field crop
33. Western border state (abbr.)

## GEORGIA CROSSWORD PUZZLE

**ACROSS**
1. Northern mountains
8. Founder of Girl Scouts: Juliette ____
11. ____ trees cover most of state
12. An important fruit crop
13. Large bird refuge: Okefenokee ____
14. Field crop
17. Southern border state (abbr.)
19. Field crop
20. Another name for peanuts
22. State flower: Cherokee ____
24. Vegetable crop: ____ potato
25. Coastal water catch
26. State abbr.
27. A building stone

*peach*

# GEORGIA

NAME _____ DATE _____

## GEORGIA WORD SEARCHING

**DIRECTIONS**
Find these hidden Georgia words (the words not in parentheses) in the grid. They can go up, down, across, at an angle, forward, or backward.

Rivers:
    Altamaha
    Chattahoochee
    Flint
    Savannah
Early Indians:
    Mound (Builders)
    Creek
Large cities:
    Atlanta
    Macon
    Athens
    Augusta
    Columbus
Important crops:
    tobacco
    peach
    peanut
    pecan
    corn
    sweet (potatoes)
Important farm products:
    broilers  (young chickens)
    eggs
    hogs
    milk
Trees:
    (black) tupelo
    cedar
    hickory
    tulip
    (sweet) gum
    walnut

| P | A | H | F | P | L | B | T | N | B | D | H | T |
|---|---|---|---|---|---|---|---|---|---|---|---|---|
| E | C | O | L | U | M | B | U | S | R | T | R | U |
| A | H | G | S | G | O | C | P | U | O | M | E | L |
| N | A | S | A | S | V | B | E | M | I | L | K | I |
| U | T | K | I | L | A | D | L | H | L | S | Y | P |
| T | T | W | M | D | T | W | O | J | E | N | H | O |
| S | A | V | A | N | N | A | H | A | R | E | C | N |
| W | H | K | D | U | I | L | M | B | S | H | R | U |
| E | O | G | F | O | L | N | G | A | P | T | T | J |
| E | O | U | P | M | F | U | O | B | H | A | J | Y |
| T | C | M | S | C | E | T | P | E | C | A | N | R |
| L | H | Y | A | W | R | I | E | A | G | T | L | O |
| K | E | E | R | C | T | B | A | F | M | L | E | K |
| H | E | G | W | Q | O | N | C | E | D | A | R | C |
| U | G | G | P | F | R | N | H | M | D | N | K | I |
| R | C | S | B | O | C | C | A | B | O | T | O | H |
| T | A | L | C | A | T | S | U | G | U | A | S | D |

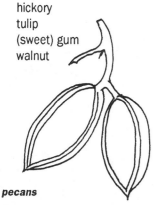

*pecans*

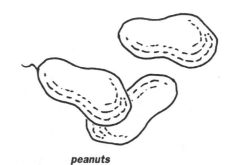

*peanuts*

From *States of Wonder* published by GoodYearBooks. Copyright © 1992 Jeanne Cheyney and Arnold Cheyney.

# HAWAII

26. Hawaiian word for "feast"
27. Truck farm crop
28. Farm animals

**DOWN**
1. Important crop
2. Hawaii consists of 132 _____.
4. Important Hawaiian food
6. Most important ocean fish
7. *Aloha* means _____.
9. The Hawaiian alphabet has _____ letters.
10. Vegetable crop
11. Starchy food made from the underground stem of the taro plant
12. State abbr.
13. The people eat much _____.
14. _____ formed the islands.
16. A fruit crop
18. The _____ ocean surrounds the islands.
21. A fruit crop
23. Orchid capital of the world

*hula dancer*

## HAWAII CROSSWORD PUZZLE

**ACROSS**
1. Original settlers
3. Most important crop: _____ cane
5. Crop: Macadamia _____
8. Some of the population is from _____
13. Honolulu: chief _____ port
15. _____ bring much money to the islands.
17. Visitors can watch _____ dancers.
19. Called "The _____ State"
20. Farm animals
22. Capital and largest city
24. Capital is located on _____ island
25. Wreaths of flowers strung together are called _____.

From *States of Wonder* published by GoodYearBooks. Copyright © 1992 Jeanne Cheyney and Arnold Cheyney.

NAME _____     DATE _____

## HAWAII FOOD PAIRS

### DIRECTIONS

All of the food names in the center oval are in pairs, except one. Write the name of each food pair on a blank. (Cross them off in the oval as you find them.) Then find the name of the food that has no pair and write it in the box.

CORN CATTLE BANANAS
NUTS RICE CABBAGE AVOCADO BEANS
PAPAYA SUGAR POULTRY TARO RICE SUGAR
HOGS POTATOES POI POTATOES CABBAGE
GUAVA BANANAS PINEAPPLE HOGS CORN PAPAYA COFFEE
CATTLE NUTS TUNA PINEAPPLE POULTRY
AVOCADO BEANS TUNA
TARO BEANS COFFEE GUAVA

_____     _____
_____     _____
_____     _____
_____     _____
_____     _____
_____     _____
_____     [                    ]

## HAWAII SCRAMBLED WORDS

### DIRECTIONS

Unscramble the words and write the answers on the lines provided. (Use scrap paper to work out your answers.)

1. There are United States **L T M Y R I I A   A S S B E** on Hawaii. _____   _____

2. In 1941, Pearl Harbor Navy Base was **M D E O B B** by the Japanese. _____

3. Some of the beach sand is **K L B A C**. _____

4.  Most of the **O P P E E L** live on the island of Oahu. _____

5. Some Hawaiian farm animals are **E A T L C T** and **S O G H**. _____   _____

6. Many **R O L E W S F** are grown and sold. _____

7. Some farmers grow **F E O C E F**. _____

8. **E S N B A** and **N A A B A N S** are grown and sold. _____   _____

## HAWAII WORDS IN WORDS

How many words can you make from the letters in "Captain James Cook," a British explorer who landed in Hawaii in 1778? (Trading with Europe followed this discovery.)

### CAPTAIN JAMES COOK

1. _____   5. _____   9. _____   13. _____

2. _____   6. _____   10. _____   14. _____

3. _____   7. _____   11. _____

4. _____   8. _____   12. _____

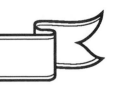

NAME _____   DATE _____

29. Mountain range: _____ Mts.
32. State tree: Western white _____
34. A river: St. _____
35. Largest _____ mine in the U.S.
36. A field crop

**DOWN**
1. _____ was discovered in 1960.
2. Eastern border state (abbr.)
3. A field crop
4. Capital and largest city
5. Called "The _____ State"
6. Most important farm animals _____
8. Falls higher than Niagara Falls
9. Factories produce _____ from trees
10. _____ cover 40 percent of Idaho.
11. Dairy-farm product
13. World-famous springs: _____ Springs
17. Weird rock formations: Cities of _____
18. Sharp, bare granite mountains
22. A field crop: sugar _____
24. A meadow flower
25. _____: most beautiful mountains
26. _____ and Clark: first white men to explore Idaho
30. A western border state (abbr.)
31. The Crystal Ice _____ has a frozen river.
33. Large wild animal

## IDAHO CROSSWORD PUZZLE

**ACROSS**
7. Most famous important crop
12. State bird: mountain _____ bird
14. A leader in _____ mining
15. Large, wild animal
16. Southern border state (abbr.)
19. A western border state (abbr.)
20. Famous ski resort: _____ Valley
21. Historic fur-trading post: _____ Hall
23. _____ Canyon: deepest canyon in North America
27. Eastern border state (abbr.)
28. Idaho never has a _____ shortage.

From *States of Wonder* published by GoodYearBooks. Copyright © 1992 Jeanne Cheyney and Arnold Cheyney.

# IDAHO

NAME _____ DATE _____

## IDAHO CLUE

### DIRECTIONS
Each set of lines has a vowel to help you determine the correct answer. All the words tell about Idaho.

Forest trees:

_ e _ _ _

_ _ _ _ _ e

_ e _ _ _

_ _ _ e _

_ i _ _

_ i _

_ i _ _ _

Chief rivers:

_ _ a _ _ _

_ a _ _ _ _

Wild animals:

_ e _ _

_ _ _ e _

_ e _ _ _

_ _ _ _ e

_ _ _ _ o _ _

_ o _ _ _

_ o _ _ _ _

_ o _ _ _ _

Cities:

_ _ _ _ _    _’ A _ _ _ _

_ a _ _ _

_ _ _ _ _    _ a _ _ _

_ _ _ _ a _ _ _

An abandoned mining town:

_ _ o _ _    _ _ _ _

Early Indian tribes:

_ _ o _ _ _ _ _

_ _ _ _ o _ _

## IDAHO SAME FIRST LETTER

### DIRECTIONS
The circled letter is the first letter for each answer. Example:

(P)  i  e
     <u>DESSERT</u>
     u  p  p  y
     <u>YOUNG DOG</u>

(B) _ _ _ _   <u>CITY</u>
    _ _ _ _ _ _ _ _   <u>CITY</u>

(C) _ _ _ _ _ _ _ _ _   <u>NATIONAL FOREST</u>
    _ _ _ _ _ _ _ _ _   <u>NATIONAL FOREST</u>

(S) _ _ _ _ _ _   <u>RIVER</u>
    _ _ _ _ _ _   <u>RIVER</u>

(C) _ _ _ _ _ _ _   <u>NATIONAL FOREST</u>
    _ _ _ _ _ _ _   <u>NATIONAL FOREST</u>

(B) _ _ _ _ _ _   <u>RIVER</u>
    _ _ _ _ _ _   <u>RIVER</u>

(P) _ _ _ _ _   <u>LAKE</u>
    _ _ _ _ _   <u>LAKE</u>

*rafting*

NAME _____    DATE _____

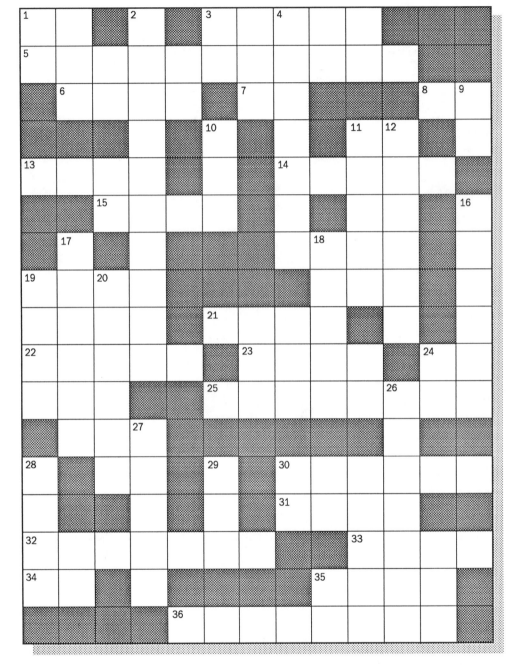

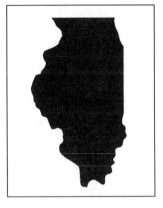

30. Leading producer of
    _____ engines
31. Illinois is part of the
    corn _____.
32. More than half of
    Illinois people live in
    _____.
33. Valuable farm animals:
    _____ cattle
34. Southern border state
    (abbr.)
35. Chief field crop
36. Leads U.S. in raising
    _____

**DOWN**
2. State has largest _____
   coal beds in the U.S.
4. State called "Land of
   _____"
9. State abbr.
10. A field crop
11. A fruit crop
12. Important tree
16. A field crop
17. State flower: Native
    _____
18. Most valuable fruit crop
19. Most important farm
    animals
20. The first settlers were
    probably from _____.
24. Western border state
    (abbr.)
26. The Mississippi River
    forms the entire _____
    border of Illinois.
27. Lake and river fish
28. Wild game bird
29. A river: _____ Muddy
    River

## ILLINOIS CROSSWORD PUZZLE

**ACROSS**
1. A western border state
   (abbr.)
3. A fruit crop
5. Capital city

6. A field crop
7. Eastern border state
   (abbr.)
8. Northern border state
   (abbr.)
13. Illinois produces much
    _____ machinery.
14. _____ freighters sail to
    Illinois ports.

15. _____ destroyed much
    of Chicago in 1871.
21. Lake and river fish
22. Largest U.S. factory for
    making _____ bottles
23. Important dairy product
25. Illinois _____ links the
    Mississippi River to the
    Gulf of Mexico.

From States of Wonder published by GoodYearBooks. Copyright © 1992 Jeanne Cheyney and Arnold Cheyney.

# ILLINOIS

NAME _____    DATE _____

## ILLINOIS NUMBER CODE

### DIRECTIONS
Look at the numbers under each line. Find the matching number in the code box and write the letters on the answer line.

| | |
|---|---|
| A – 1 | |
| B – 2 | |
| C – 3 | |
| D – 4 | |
| E – 5 | |
| F – 6 | |
| G – 7 | |
| H – 8 | |
| I – 9 | |
| J – 10 | |
| K – 11 | |
| L – 12 | |
| M – 13 | |
| N – 14 | |
| O – 15 | |
| P – 16 | |
| Q – 17 | |
| R – 18 | |
| S – 19 | |
| T – 20 | |
| U – 21 | |
| V – 22 | |
| W – 23 | |
| X – 24 | |
| Y – 25 | |
| Z – 26 | |

*corn*

**1. Whose home is in Galena?**

__20__ __8__ __5__   __8__ __15__ __13__ __5__   __15__ __6__   __21__ __12__ __25__ __19__ __19__ __5__ __19__   __19__ .

__7__ __18__ __1__ __14__ __20__ ,  __18__  __20__ __8__   __21__ __19__   __16__ __18__ __5__ __19__ __9__ __4__ __5__ __14__ __20__

**2. Which recent U.S. President was born in Illinois?**

__18__ __15__ __14__ __1__ __12__ __4__   __18__ __5__ __1__ __7__ __1__ __14__

**3. What archeological site can be seen in Illinois?**

__4__ __9__ __3__ __11__ __19__ __15__ __14__   __13__ __15__ __21__ __14__ __4__ __19__ :   __16__ __1__ __18__ __20__ __12__ __25__

__15__ __16__ __5__ __14__ __5__ __4__   __9__ __14__ __4__ __9__ __1__ __14__   __13__ __15__ __21__ __14__ __4__ __19__   __23__ __9__ __20__ __8__

__9__ __14__ __4__ __9__ __1__ __14__   __19__ __11__ __5__ __12__ __5__ __20__ __15__ __14__ __19__

**4. Of what is Illinois a large producer?**

__6__ __1__ __18__ __13__   __13__ __1__ __3__ __8__ __9__ __14__ __5__ __18__ __25__

**5. Illinois is a leading producer of what?**

__4__ __9__ __5__ __19__ __5__ __12__   __5__ __14__ __7__ __9__ __14__ __5__ __19__

**6. What is the name of the city where Abraham Lincoln lived?**

__8__ __5__   __12__ __9__ __22__ __5__ __4__   __9__ __14__   __19__ __16__ __18__ __9__ __14__ __7__ __6__ __9__ __5__ __12__ __4__ .

*farm machinery*

27

NAME _____     DATE _____

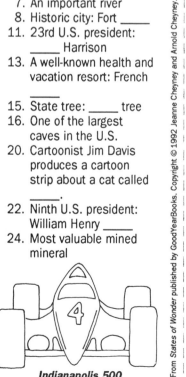

29. Eastern border state (abbr.)
30. Along Lake Michigan: famous sand _____
31. A famous town: _____ Claus

**DOWN**
1. Northern border state (abbr.)
2. Indiana poet: James Whitcomb _____
3. A valuable hardwood tree
4. A city: Terre _____
5. Western border state (abbr.)
7. An important river
8. Historic city: Fort _____
11. 23rd U.S. president: _____ Harrison
13. A well-known health and vacation resort: French _____
15. State tree: _____ tree
16. One of the largest caves in the U.S.
20. Cartoonist Jim Davis produces a cartoon strip about a cat called _____.
22. Ninth U.S. president: William Henry _____
24. Most valuable mined mineral

## INDIANA CROSSWORD PUZZLE

**ACROSS**
6. Capital and largest city
8. A river: _____ River
9. State abbr.
10. A tree
12. Indiana has _____ refineries.
14. State flower
17. A bird: Blue_____
18. A southern border state (abbr.)
19. An important river
21. Huge northern border lake
23. A wild flower
24. Chief field crop
25. Bird seen on prairies and near swamps: prairie _____
26. Called "The _____ State"
27. A river
28. A river: St. _____

28

*Indianapolis 500*

From *States of Wonder* published by GoodYearBooks. Copyright © 1992 Jeanne Cheyney and Arnold Cheyney.

# I N D I A N A

NAME _____ DATE _____

## INDIANA SUPPLY THE VOWEL

### DIRECTIONS

Look for the following words in the grid (the words not in parentheses). The words can go up, down, across, at angles, backward, or forward. Parts of words may overlap. Supply the correct vowel—*a e i o u*—for the center of each word group.

White (river)
oak (tree)
coal
(prairie) lark (bird)
oil
Ohio (southern border river)
oriole (bird)
pussy (willows, a spring plant)
quail
thrush (bird)
cardinal (state bird)
wren
Raggedy (Ann: a doll created in Indianapolis)
Tecumseh (Indian chief)
tomato (valuable crop)
hickory
Tippecanoe (a river and an 1811 battle)
violet
apples (leading fruit crop)

| B | S | R | O | L | V | P | D | A | H | U | M | C |
|---|---|---|---|---|---|---|---|---|---|---|---|---|
| H | T | H | M | W | J | Y | A | G | E | F | T | L |
| V | O | O | L | E | T | B | E | N | S | N | I | O |
| O | P | C | O | K | I | C | Q | P | M | A | R | S |
| Y | P | U | K | W | P | I | H | S | O | R | H | T |
| C | E | D | E | O | H | O | X | Q | C | S | I | O |
| K | C | G | W | C | R | G | D | J | E | B | S | H |
| L | A | V | M | H | C | Y | F | E | T | O | W | Y |
| H | N | D | L | V | I | S | L | Y | X | A | I | P |
| U | O | F | A | M | D | T | N | S | R | H | N | G |
| G | E | F | N | L | Y | D | O | G | G | A | R | K |
| I | V | N | I | C | B | L | R | E | Z | B | X | O |
| F | J | A | D | K | P | J | W | S | F | O | R | V |
| K | A | L | R | P | A | N | C | H | E | I | W | T |
| T | O | M | O | T | O | X | U | C | O | A | L | M |
| A | C | Z | C | R | M | L | T | L | A | I | C | Y |
| B | M | P | W | Z | K | A | E | B | K | D | L | A |

**Raggedy
Ann
invented**

*canoeing*

NAME _____    DATE _____

36. A tree: White _____
38. A vegetable crop

**DOWN**
1. _____ City
2. The "first-place recognition" in U.S. corn production goes _____ and forth between the states of Iowa and Illinois.
3. A leading animal industry: _____yards
4. Birthplace of the 31st president: Herbert _____
8. About 10 percent of the people live on _____.
11. A tree
12. Capital and largest city: Des _____
13. A western border state (abbr.)
14. Eastern boundary river
15. Largest U.S. _____ processing plant: Sioux City
18. Norman Borlaug got the Nobel Peace _____ in 1970.
19. Large city: _____ Rapids
20. Important field crop
25. Chief fruit crop
26. An eastern border state (abbr.)
27. Iowa is called "The _____ State"
31. A leading animal industry: _____packing
32. State bird: Gold _____
33. Famous rural artist: Grant _____
35. Northern border state (abbr.)
37. An eastern border state (abbr.)

## IOWA CROSSWORD PUZZLE

**ACROSS**
1. An important crop
5. Large river
6. Stream fish: _____fish
7. Most important field crop
9. Southern border state (abbr.)
10. Leading U.S. state for raising _____ (animal)
16. A field crop
17. River on most of west boundary
21. State flower: Wild _____
22. Cedar Rapids: large _____ mills
23. State abbr.
24. Important field crop
28. A western border state (abbr.)
29. A tree
30. Important dairy product
34. Important farm animals: _____ cattle

# IOWA

NAME _____ DATE _____

## IOWA SKYSCRAPER

### DIRECTIONS

Write your answers in the boxes. The circled letters will help you.

1. Abbr. for river
2. Iowa abbr.
3. Wild animal
4. An Indian chief: Black _____
5. Cover about 93 percent of the state
6. Small wild animal
7. Iowa: called "The _____ State"
8. Wild flower
9. State bird
10. Tree
11. River

## IOWA ALPHABET SEARCH

### DIRECTIONS

Find at least four names of Iowa rivers, cities and towns, crops, flowers, and trees that have letters of the alphabet used only once in each *individual* word. Example: Des Moines (yes, because the letters are used only once in each individual word).

Crops

_____
_____
_____
_____

Flowers

_____
_____
_____
_____

Trees

_____
_____
_____
_____

Rivers

_____
_____
_____

Towns, Cities

_____
_____
_____
_____

hogs

## IOWA WORDS IN WORDS

How many words can you make from the letters in "Herbert Hoover," the 31st U.S. President? (He was born in Iowa.)

### HERBERT HOOVER

1. _____
2. _____
3. _____
4. _____
5. _____
6. _____
7. _____
8. _____
9. _____
10. _____
11. _____
12. _____
13. _____
14. _____

31

NAME _____    DATE _____

31. _____ is grown to save the soil from the wind.
32. Northern border state (abbr.)
33. First permanent white settlement: _____ Leavenworth
34. Kansas lies _____ between the Atlantic and Pacific Oceans.
35. Capital city

**DOWN**
2. Important river
3. Leading U.S. crop
7. _____ once roamed the prairies.
8. A tree
10. Southern border state (abbr.)
11. _____ were once driven many miles to Dodge City.
12. A leading state in producing _____ cattle
14. Dodge City was the _____ Capital of the World.
15. Cattle were once driven many miles to _____.
16. Important field crop: _____beans
17. _____ longhorns were once important cattle.
19. Western border state (abbr.)
20. An important river
22. Wild game birds
23. Indian meaning for the word Kansas: people of the south _____
24. Largest city and manufacturing city
25. _____ was found in natural gas (1905).
26. Important dairy product
27. Famous cattle town: _____ City
29. State abbr.

## KANSAS CROSSWORD PUZZLE

**ACROSS**
1. Kansas: sometimes called "The _____ of America"
4. John _____: fought against slavery
5. _____ and movies made early Kansas famous.
6. Home of former President Eisenhower: _____
9. Famous Dodge City lawman: Wyatt _____
13. Kansas was named for the _____ Indians.
18. Called "The _____ State"
21. Eastern border state (abbr.)
27. Small animal: Prairie _____
28. Grave and museum of the 34th president: President _____
30. A tree

From *States of Wonder* published by GoodYearBooks. Copyright © 1992 Jeanne Cheyney and Arnold Cheyney.

# KANSAS

NAME _____    DATE _____

## KANSAS NAME THE STATE BIRD

**DIRECTIONS**

Fill in the dotted lines with your answers. If they are correct, the circled letters will spell the name of Kansas's state bird.

1. A famous Dodge City lawman          1. ⬤ _ _ _ _   _ _ _ _
2. State flower                        2. _ _ _ _ _ _ _ ⬤ _
3. A river for barges                  3. _ _ _ _ ⬤ _ _ _
4. Leading field crop                  4. _ _ _ _ ⬤
5. Small ground animal                 5. _ _ _ _ _ _ ⬤ _ _
6. Game bird                           6. _ _ _ _ _ ⬤ _ _   _ _ _ _ _
7. Leads U.S. in producing civilian ___   7. _ _ _ _ _ _ ⬤ _
8. Important industry in Hutchinson    8. _ _ _ _ _ _ ⬤ _ _ _ _
9. Important farm animals              9. _ ⬤ _ _   _ _ _ _ _
10. Important crop                     10. _ _ _ ⬤ _   _ _ _ _ _ _
11. A game bird                        11. _ _ _ ⬤ _
12. A river                            12. _ _ ⬤ _
13. A bird                             13. _ ⬤ _ _ _ _ _ _
14. A famous Dodge City lawman         14. _ _ _ _   _ _ ⬤ _ _ _ _ _
15. A famous Dodge City lawman         15. _ _ _   _ ⬤ _ _ _ _ _
16. A poisonous snake                  16. _ ⬤ _ _ _ _ _ _
17. A large city                       17. _ _ ⬤ _ _   _ _ _ _

## KANSAS SCRAMBLED WORDS

**DIRECTIONS**

Unscramble the words and write the answers on the lines provided. (Use scrap paper to work out your answers.) All the words tell about Kansas.

Wild flowers

  iheltts _____

  elcvor _____

  aydis _____

Birds

  noirb _____

  kahw _____

  wcor _____

Wild animals

  tiabrb _____

  carnoco _____

  tukamsr _____

*prairie dog*

33

NAME _____ DATE _____

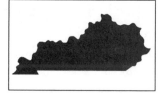

28. A northern border state (abbr.)
30. Tourist attraction: _____ Cave
31. Lake and river fish
32. Capital city
33. State abbr.
34. Important fruit crop

**DOWN**
1. State flower
2. Famous arts and crafts town
3. Famous songwriter Stephen _____ wrote "My Old Kentucky Home."
4. Largest city and Ohio River port
5. A river: _____ Fork
6. In May, horses run in the Kentucky _____.
7. A bird that eats cattle pests
8. A field crop
12. Important river
15. Eastern mountains
16. A western border state (abbr.)
19. North-boundary river
21. A field crop
23. A very important field crop
24. An eastern border state (abbr.)
25. Restored historic village: _____ Village
27. Fort _____: gold is stored underground there
29. Daniel _____ founded Boonesborough.

## KENTUCKY CROSSWORD PUZZLE

**ACROSS**
3. A state park: Cumberland _____
9. Important farm animals
10. Called "The _____ State"
11. Important dairy product
13. Important poultry product
14. An eastern border state (abbr.)
17. _____ in the Appalachian Plateau is not good for farming.
18. Born in Kentucky: 16th U.S. president
20. State leads in _____ mining
22. A tree
23. Southern border state (abbr.)
26. A northern border state (abbr.)

From *States of Wonder* published by GoodYearBooks. Copyright © 1992 Jeanne Cheyney and Arnold Cheyney.

NAME _____ DATE _____

## KENTUCKY CROSSING OVER

### DIRECTIONS

Use a pencil for this game. Find words from the following list that have the correct number of spaces and letters to fit into the crossing-over boxes (the words not in parentheses). Each word has a place where it belongs. The first word is done for you. To continue, find an 8-letter word with "o" in the fifth space, and so on. All the words tell about Kentucky.

**3 letters**
- hay
- Tug (Fork: a river)
- rye
- ash (tree)

**4 letters**
- Ohio (river)
- eggs
- pine
- beef
- corn
- milk
- oats
- Salt (river)
- (Fort) Knox
- hogs
- coal
- iris (flower)

**5 letters**
- Green (river)
- wheat
- cedar (tree)
- quail (bird)
- (Big) Sandy (river)
- (Daniel) Boone (frontiersman)
- (Cumberland) Falls
- (Jefferson) Davis (born in KY)
- (Kentucky) Derby (horse race)

**6 letters**
- barley
- apples
- violet
- Strong (City: a rodeo)
- Shaker (historic village)
- grouse (game bird)

**7 letters**
- hickory
- opossum
- (Abe) Lincoln (born in KY)
- tobacco
- Mammoth (Cave)
- Shawnee (Indians)
- peaches

- Liberty (Hall)
- Licking (R.)

**8 letters**
- Iroquois (Indians)
- soybeans
- Kentucky (river)
- Cherokee (Indians)
- broilers (young chickens)
- cardinal (state bird)

**9 letters**
- goldenrod
- buttercup
- sunflower (state flower)
- bluegrass
- Owensboro (city)
- Lexington (city)
- Tennessee (river)

**10 letters**
- (KY) coffeetree (state tree)
- pennyroyal (flower)
- Herrington (Lake)

P
E
N
N
Y
R
O
Y
A
L

35

NAME _____  DATE _____

## DOWN

1. Most important field crop
2. Important field crop
3. A type of music from historic New Orleans French Quarter
5. Western border state (abbr.)
6. Important coastal fishing catch
7. Descendants of French settlers from Canada
8. A flowering vine: _____suckle
10. World's largest indoor arena
11. Colorful flower
12. An important field crop
13. Important poultry product
14. New _____: largest city and one of the world's busiest ports
15. Wall that holds back flood waters
16. An important field crop: sugar _____
17. A wild flower
18. State tree: Bald _____
20. State capital: _____ Rouge
21. A large wild animal
22. Called "The ___ State"
24. A marsh rodent
25. Eastern border state (abbr.)

## LOUISIANA CROSSWORD PUZZLE

### ACROSS

1. Leader in mining _____
4. Important vegetable crop: sweet _____
9. Slow-moving waters at lake or river inlets and outlets
16. Descendants of French and Spanish settlers
19. State abbr.
23. Northern border state (abbr.)
26. Spanish _____ hangs from some trees.
27. Famous festival in New Orleans: _____ Gras
28. Avery Island: an _____ sanctuary
29. A tree
30. Largest lake

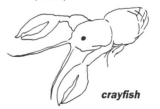

*crayfish*

From *States of Wonder* published by GoodYearBooks. Copyright © 1992 Jeanne Cheyney and Arnold Cheyney.

# LOUISIANA

NAME _____     DATE _____

## LOUISIANA CLUE

### DIRECTIONS

Each set of lines has a vowel to help you determine the correct answer. All the words tell about Louisiana.

Important rivers:

__ __ __ i __ __

__ __ __ __ __ __ i __ __

__ __ __ __ __ __ __ i __ __ __

Birds:

__ __ __ e __ __

__ __ __ __ e __ __

__ e __ __ __ __ __ __

Wild animals:

a __ __ __ __ __ __ __ __ __

__ __ a __ __ __

__ __ __ __ __ __ a __

Freshwater fish:

__ a __ __

__ a __ __ __ __

__ u __ __ __ __ __

Ocean fish:

__ a __ __

__ a __ __ __ __

**egret**

## LOUISIANA NUMBER CODE

### DIRECTIONS

Look at the number under each line. Then find the matching number in the code box and write the letters on the answer lines.

| | |
|---|---|
| A – 1 | N – 14 |
| B – 2 | O – 15 |
| C – 3 | P – 16 |
| D – 4 | Q – 17 |
| E – 5 | R – 18 |
| F – 6 | S – 19 |
| G – 7 | T – 20 |
| H – 8 | U – 21 |
| I – 9 | V – 22 |
| J – 10 | W – 23 |
| K – 11 | X – 24 |
| L – 12 | Y – 25 |
| M – 13 | Z – 26 |

1. For what is Avery Island famous?

$\overline{1}\ \overline{14}$     $\overline{5}\ \overline{7}\ \overline{18}\ \overline{5}\ \overline{20}$     ( $\overline{2}\ \overline{9}\ \overline{18}\ \overline{4}$ )

$\overline{19}\ \overline{1}\ \overline{14}\ \overline{3}\ \overline{20}\ \overline{21}\ \overline{1}\ \overline{18}\ \overline{25}$

2. Who was a famous pirate and where did he live?

$\overline{10}\ \overline{5}\ \overline{1}\ \overline{14}$     $\overline{12}\ \overline{1}\ \overline{6}\ \overline{9}\ \overline{20}\ \overline{20}\ \overline{5}$ :

$\overline{7}\ \overline{18}\ \overline{1}\ \overline{14}\ \overline{4}$     $\overline{9}\ \overline{19}\ \overline{12}\ \overline{5}$

3. Louisiana is the world's largest producer of what fish?

$\overline{3}\ \overline{18}\ \overline{1}\ \overline{25}\ \overline{6}\ \overline{9}\ \overline{19}\ \overline{8}$

**Mardi Gras**

# MAINE

NAME _____ DATE _____

13. Most important industry: _____ (manu-facturing from wood)
16. Lake and stream fish
17. Largest city
19. A chief river
21. West, north, and east border country
24. Dairy product
25. An ocean catch
26. A valuable forest tree: Balsam _____
27. Maine has many _____ yards.
28. A western border state (abbr.)
29. Small wild animal
30. Maine fishermen lead U.S. in the _____ catch.
31. Leads U.S. in producing _____ (wood product)

## DOWN
2. Capital city
4. _____ lies farther east than any U.S. city.
7. State abbr.
8. South-border ocean
10. State tree: White _____
14. Most valuable fruit crop
15. Large wild animal
18. The only national park in New England
20. Leads U.S. in packing _____ (a fish)
22. Most important vegetable crop
23. Patent for first ear _____ (1877)

## MAINE CROSSWORD PUZZLE

### ACROSS
1. Maine is one of the states in the area called "New _____."
3. NW mountain range: _____ Mts.
5. West _____ Head, a small peninsula, is the most eastern U.S. piece of land.
6. Important poultry product
9. _____ land covers nearly 90 percent of the state.
11. There are thousands of _____ along the coastline.
12. In many places along the coast, _____ blink warnings to ships.

From *States of Wonder* published by GoodYearBooks. Copyright © 1992 Jeanne Cheyney and Arnold Cheyney.

# MAINE

## MAINE WORD SEARCHING

**DIRECTIONS**

Find these hidden Maine words in the grid (the words not in parentheses). They can go up, down, across, at an angle, forward, or backward.

Largest lake:
    Moosehead
Tourist attraction:
    (Kennebunk) wedding
      (cake house)
Wood products:
    (ice cream) sticks
    matches
    canoes
    toys
    skis
    boxes
    (lobster) traps
State bird:
    chickadee
Valuable trees:
    (balsam) fir
    basswood
    beech
    hemlock
    birch
    maple
    oak
    spruce
Chief rivers:
    Androscoggin
    Saco
Important rivers:
    Kennebec
    Penobscot

| R | B | A | S | B | S | G | N | I | D | D | E | W |
|---|---|---|---|---|---|---|---|---|---|---|---|---|
| D | I | X | B | T | F | Q | D | S | Y | F | B | N |
| A | R | H | N | R | O | B | J | I | G | X | I | A |
| E | C | W | M | A | P | L | E | K | Q | G | C | R |
| H | H | K | E | P | M | H | W | S | G | T | H | O |
| E | S | E | K | S | J | P | L | O | O | N | I | K |
| S | K | P | M | B | E | E | C | H | Z | M | C | A |
| O | C | K | P | L | T | S | F | J | N | I | K | E |
| O | I | P | E | N | O | B | S | C | O | T | A | G |
| M | T | K | S | R | Y | C | Z | Y | W | A | D | E |
| X | S | E | D | S | S | A | K | I | F | O | E | S |
| S | L | N | G | E | Y | Z | V | T | O | C | E | O |
| P | A | N | B | O | X | E | S | W | F | H | D | S |
| R | X | E | C | N | Z | N | S | S | C | O | A | F |
| U | P | B | O | A | K | S | E | T | J | C | I | A |
| C | E | E | J | C | A | L | A | H | D | A | O | B |
| E | M | C | Q | B | R | M | Y | D | K | S | H | V |

From *States of Wonder* published by GoodYearBooks. Copyright © 1992 Jeanne Cheyney and Arnold Cheyney.

**lobster**

*sardines*

39

NAME _____     DATE _____

17. Important dairy product
18. The _____ Mountains cover the northwest strip of Maryland.
20. Farm animals
21. Most valuable mined mineral: crushed _____
26. Maryland is divided in two parts: Eastern Shore and _____ Shore.
27. Playful, water-loving fur animal
28. A _____ connects eastern and western Maryland.
29. A forest tree
30. A tree
31. _____ cover 40 percent of the state.
32. A leading U.S. fishing catch
33. Important field crop: _____ crop
34. Southwestern border state (abbr.)

**DOWN**
2. Capital city
3. A fruit crop
4. A large wild animal
7. U.S. capital, _____ D.C., is on the state border
15. Largest city and important seaport
19. A river fish
22. Maryland has over 150 kinds of _____.
23. _____: a leading U.S. fishing catch
24. State's chief poultry product
25. Important field crop

## MARYLAND CROSSWORD PUZZLE

**ACROSS**
1. Important bay cutting through the state
5. Called "The Old _____ State"
6. Northern border state (abbr.)
8. State flower: Black-eyed _____
9. Most common tree
10. State abbr.
11. Annapolis: home of the U.S. _____ Academy
12. Eastern border state (abbr.)
13. Francis Scott _____ wrote "The Star Spangled Banner" in 1814.
14. A field crop
16. Most valuable field product

From *States of Wonder* published by GoodYearBooks. Copyright © 1992 Jeanne Cheyney and Arnold Cheyney.

NAME _____     DATE _____

## MARYLAND RIVER AND CREEK PAIRS

### DIRECTIONS

All of the river and creek names in the oval are in pairs, except one. Write the name of each river and creek pair on a blank. (Cross them off in the oval as you find them.) Then find the name of the river or creek that has no pair and write it in the box.

Oval word list: CONOCOCHEAGUE, ANTIETAM, ELK, CHESTER, POTOMAC, WICOMICO, SEVERN, NORTHEAST, SOUTH, CHOPTANK, ELK, MONOCRACY, SUSQUEHANNA, SASSAFRAS, PATUXENT, SASSAFRAS, GUNPOWDER, POTOMAC, CHOPTANK, SEVERN, NANTICOKE, CONOCOCHEAGUE, WICOMICO, SOUTH, SUSQUEHANNA, ANTIETAM, CHESTER, NANTICOKE, YOUGHIOGHENY, GUNPOWDER, PATUXENT, YOUGHIOGHENY, MONOCRACY

_____   _____

_____   _____

_____   _____

_____   _____

_____   _____

_____   _____

_____   _____

[ box ]

_____   _____

## MARYLAND SCRAMBLED WORDS

*otter*

### DIRECTIONS

Unscramble the words and write the answers on the lines provided. (Use scrap paper to work out your answers.)

1. In Maryland, striped bass are called **C S H O I R F K**. _____

2. (1862) Antietam is a **V L I C I   R W A   F T A L D L I B T E E**. _____ _____ _____

3. 1634: Maryland's first colonial **E E E T T N S L T M** was in **T S   A S Y M R   I Y T C**. _____ :

_____ _____ _____

4. **S O T E E M G S N** are mined in Maryland. _____

5. 1828: The first **R B L L E U A M** factory in the U.S. _____

6. Wye Mills has the largest **H E T W I   A K O   R E E T** in the U.S. _____ _____ _____

7. Frederick: home of Barbara Fritchie, who defied **E F D R O E E C A N T** army forces. _____

## MARYLAND WORDS IN WORDS

How many words can you make from the letters in "Umbrella Factory"? (In 1828, Maryland had the first factory in the U.S. to make umbrellas.)

### UMBRELLA FACTORY

1. _____   5. _____   9. _____

2. _____   6. _____   10. _____

3. _____   7. _____   11. _____

4. _____   8. _____   12. _____

*clam*

# MASSACHUSETTS

NAME _____     DATE _____

18. Birthplace of the second U.S. President: John ___
22. New _____: important fishing and fish-canning port
24. Boston _____ Party: men dressed like Indians and threw boxes overboard
26. Massachusetts leads U.S. states in producing _____ (a fruit)
29. A northern border state (abbr.)
30. Chief field crop

**DOWN**
1. Called "The ____ State"
2. The Pilgrims landed in _____ in 1620.
3. Alexander Graham Bell invented the _____ in 1876.
5. A poultry product
8. A river
9. An important dairy product
11. The Massachusetts coast has many excellent _____.
15. Both _____ and volleyball were invented in MA.
16. The Revolutionary _____ began in 1775.
17. A large resort island
19. A valuable coastal fish: ____fish
20. A national historic site: _____ Iron Works
21. Birthplace of 35th U.S. President: John F. _____
23. Large wild animal
25. The first ____paper was published in MA.
26. A peninsula and famous resort: Cape _____
27. A southern border state (abbr.)
28. A northern border state (abbr.)

## MASSACHUSETTS CROSSWORD PUZZLE

**ACROSS**
1. Capital and largest city
2. Most valuable agricultural product: greenhouse and nursery ___
4. The ____ (fishing) catch is the most valuable in the U.S.
6. Western border state (abbr.)
7. State tree: American ____
10. Valuable fishing catch
11. The first U.S. public ____ school opened in 1821.
12. The first ____ Office was opened in 1639.
13. ____men fought the first Revolutionary War battle in 1775.
14. A southern border state (abbr.)

From States of Wonder published by GoodYearBooks. Copyright © 1992 Jeanne Cheyney and Arnold Cheyney.

# MASSACHUSETTS

From *States of Wonder* published by GoodYearBooks. Copyright © 1992 Jeanne Cheyney and Arnold Cheyney.

NAME _____     DATE _____

## MASSACHUSETTS NAME THE SPECIAL DAY

### DIRECTIONS
Fill in the dotted lines with your answers. If they are correct, the letters will spell the name of a special day.

1. Western hills
2. One of the first Revolutionary War battles
3. Most important coastal river
4. Most important river
5. State bird
6. A town of historic witch trials
7. Important fishing port
8. An 1812 ship docked at the Boston Navy Yard
9. A man who warned the people that the British were coming
10. A good dairy-farm area
11. A large island
12. The highest point in MA

1. ◯ _ _ _ _ _ _
2. _ _ _ _ _ _ ◯ _ _ _ _
3. _ _ _ _ _ _ ◯ _ _ _
4. _ _ _ ◯ _ _ _ _ _ _
5. _ _ _ _ ◯ _ _
6. _ _ _ ◯ _
7. _ _ _ _ ◯ _ _ _ _ _ _ _
8. _ _ _ _ _ _ ◯ _ _ _ _ _
9. _ _ _ _ ◯ _ _ _ _
10. _ _ _ _ _ ◯ _ _ _ _ _ _
11. _ _ _ _ _ _ _ _ ◯ _ _ _ _ _ _
12. _ _ ◯ _ _ _ _ _ _ _

## MASSACHUSETTS ALPHABET SEARCH

### DIRECTIONS
Find names of Massachusetts rivers, fish, trees, towns, and cities that have letters of the alphabet used only once in each *individual* word.

| Rivers | Fish | Trees | Towns and Cities |
|---|---|---|---|
| _____ | _____ | _____ | _____ |
| _____ | _____ | _____ | _____ |
| _____ | _____ | _____ | _____ |
| _____ | _____ | _____ | _____ |

### DIRECTIONS
Find names of Massachusetts rivers, fish, and wild animals that have letters of the alphabet used *more than* once in each word.

| Rivers | Fish | Wild animals |
|---|---|---|
| _____ | _____ | _____ |
| _____ | _____ | _____ |
| _____ | _____ | _____ |
| _____ | _____ | _____ |

*cranberries*

**43**

NAME _____     DATE _____

16. A small animal known for its fur
17. Most important dairy product
19. State bird
20. Battle Creek: "_____ Bowl of America"
22. Farm animals: cattle and _____
24. A vegetable crop
25. An important fruit
26. Hatcheries produce _____.
27. An important field crop: _____ crop
28. Farm animals
30. An important fruit: _____ crop
31. An important food from insects and fruit-tree flowers (food)
32. Milk: important _____ product

## DOWN
1. _____ cover more than half of the state.
2. Largest city and automobile capital
3. State leads in growing _____ (vegetable)
6. Very busy ship canals: _____ canals
7. _____ Bridge, 5 miles long, connects both parts of the state.
11. State capital
18. An important fruit
21. An important fruit: the _____ crop
23. An important fruit: the _____ crop
29. A southern border state (abbr.)

## MICHIGAN CROSSWORD PUZZLE

### ACROSS
1. Henry _____ built a workable car in 1896.
2. Farm hatcheries raise _____ (poultry).
4. A tree
5. Michigan touches four of the Great Lakes: _____, Huron, Michigan, and Superior.
6. An important mined mineral
7. State abbr.
8. A hardwood tree
9. Southern border state (abbr.)
10. Michigan: leader in making _____
12. Wild animal: black _____
13. An automaking center: _____ (city)
14. State tree: White _____
15. An important fruit crop

From *States of Wonder* published by GoodYearBooks. Copyright © 1992 Jeanne Cheyney and Arnold Cheyney.

NAME _____     DATE _____

## MICHIGAN MORSE CODE

### DIRECTIONS

Look at the dots and dashes under each line. Then find the matching dots and dashes in the code box and write the code letters on the answer lines.

| | |
|---|---|
| A | .− |
| B | −... |
| C | −.−. |
| D | −.. |
| E | . |
| F | ..−. |
| G | −−. |
| H | .... |
| I | .. |
| J | .−−− |
| K | −.− |
| L | .−.. |
| M | −− |
| N | −. |
| O | −−− |
| P | .−−. |
| Q | −−.− |
| R | .−. |
| S | ... |
| T | − |
| U | ..− |
| V | ...− |
| W | .−− |
| X | −..− |
| Y | −.−− |
| Z | −−.. |

1. Michigan was the first state to have something. What was it?

___ .... .   .−. .−. .− ___   −−. .− ___ . − .   ...

___ .−. .− ... .−.. −.−.   .−.. . − . .− . .   −−− −.

___ ___ ___ ___ ___ ___ ___ ___

... − .−. − .−   ___ ...

2. What is Michigan called? Why?

"   ___ .... .   .−− −−− .−.. ...− . .−. . −. .   .

___ ...   .−− −−− ... ...   .−.. .. −. . .−. .   ___ ___ ___ ... −.   .

.−. −.−. ...−   .−.− −.. . ...   −.−   ___ .−. .− .   .−. . .− −−.

... ...   ___ ___   ___ .−. .−   ... .− .   −−−

3. What does the auto factory in Wixam use for welding car bodies together?

.−. −−− ___.. −−− − ...

cherries

4. What makes the Bissell Company in Grand Rapids famous?

.−. .− ...− .   −− .− −.−. . .− .−. ...   ___ ...

.−. .− .− ... −   ...   −− .− ... . ...   .−.

___   . .− ... − .   ... .−. .   ...

5. Michigan has great numbers of what animal?

___ ___ −.. . . .−.

6. Michigan is formed into two peninsulas separated by water. What connects them?

___ ___ ___ ___ ___ ___ ___ ___

−− .− −.−. .. −. .− .− −.−. .   .−.. .. −. −.− ... −−− ...

Ford

45

# MINNESOTA

NAME _____     DATE _____

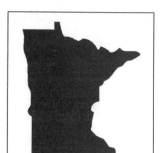

22. MN produces much
    _____ from wheat.
25. A vegetable crop
27. Important field crop
28. Wild animal: black
    _____
29. State tree: Norway _____
30. MN produces 70% of
    U.S. _____ ore.
31. Important vegetable
    crop: dry _____
32. Eastern border state
    (abbr.)
34. A leading U.S. state in
    making _____ (dairy
    product)
35. Largest city

**DOWN**
1. Years ago, many fur-
   bearing animals
   attracted fur _____.
2. A vegetable crop: green
   _____
4. Called "The _____ State"
5. State capital: St. _____
7. Minneapolis and St.
   Paul: _____ cities.
8. The Mississippi River
   begins in Lake _____.
12. An important _____-
    making state (dairy
    product)
17. Busiest fresh-water port
    in North America
19. A U.S. leader in this
    dairy product: _____
23. Most important field
    crop
24. Cellophane transparent
    _____ invented in MN.
26. Most important fruit
    crop
33. State abbr.

## MINNESOTA CROSSWORD PUZZLE

**ACROSS**

3. A leading U.S. state in
   raising _____ (farm
   animals)
6. Famous medical center:
   _____ Clinic

9. Northern border country
10. A western border state
    (abbr.)
11. Important field crop
13. A field crop
14. A western border state
    (abbr.)
15. A field crop: sugar _____
16. Southern border state

(abbr.)
18. Minnesota has the most
    _____ area of any state.
19. In "The Song of
    Hiawatha," Longfellow
    wrote about _____ Falls.
20. Produces much
    soybean _____
21. Largest lake: _____ Lake

From *States of Wonder* published by GoodYearBooks. Copyright © 1992 Jeanne Cheyney and Arnold Cheyney.

# MINNESOTA

NAME _____ DATE _____

## MINNESOTA CLUE

### DIRECTIONS
Each set of lines has a vowel to help you determine the correct answer. All the words tell about Minnesota.

Cities:

__ a __ __ __   __ __ __ __ __ __

__ a __ __ __ __

__ __ __   __ a __ __ __

__ a __   __ __ __ __ __

__ __ a __ __   __ __ __ __

Early Indian tribes:

__ i __ __ __

__ __ __ i __ __ __ __ __

Big lakes:

__ i __ __ __ __ __ __ __

__ i __ __ __ __ __ __ __ __ __ __ __ __

__ i __   __ __ __ __ __ __

National forests:

__ __ i __ __ __ __ __

__ __ __ __ __ __ i __ __

Rivers:

__ __ o __   __ __ __ __

o __ __ __ __ __   __ __ __ __

__ __ __ __   __ o __ __

Big wild animals:

__ __ __ __ e

__ __ __ __ __ __   __ e __ __

__ e __ __

bear

## MINNESOTA SKYSCRAPER

### DIRECTIONS
Write your answers in the boxes. The circled letters will help you.

1. Minnesota abbr.
2. The largest lake
3. Minnesota has about 900,000 milk _____.
4. A river
5. A nut tree: black _____
6. A restored pioneer village: Murphy's _____
7. A restored 1820 fort: Fort _____
8. A beautiful old mansion in Duluth
9. Brainerd: _____ racing at the Raceway
10. Home _____ were invented in Minnesota. (They are used to control the heat or cool air in homes.)

## MINNESOTA WORDS IN WORDS

How many words can you make from the letters in "Bread and Butter State," one of Minnesota's nicknames?

### BREAD AND BUTTER STATE

1. _____
2. _____
3. _____
4. _____
5. _____
6. _____
7. _____
8. _____
9. _____
10. _____

47

# MISSISSIPPI

NAME _____ DATE _____

20. The Mississippi R. changed its course and formed the _____ lakes.
21. A slow-moving stream
22. Important field crop
25. Most important coastal fishing catch
27. A tree
30. A field crop
31. Petrified Forest: giant stone _____
32. An important poultry product
33. Capital and largest city

## DOWN
2. An important field crop
3. A steam-powered boat that travels on the Mississippi R.: _____ Queen
5. A western border state (abbr.)
7. The chief field crop: _____ crop
8. A south-boundary body of water: Gulf of _____
10. An important vegetable: _____ potato
11. National Civil War Battlefield
12. Important fish industry: _____ fish farms
15. A western border state (abbr.)
17. Chief shrimp-packing port
23. Important hatchery (poultry)
24. Hardwood tree
26. Important nut tree
28. A field crop
29. Important farm animals

## MISSISSIPPI CROSSWORD PUZZLE

### ACROSS
1. Singer Elvis _____ was born in Tupelo.
4. Eastern border state (abbr.)
6. A river: _____ Sunflower
8. Called "The _____ State"
9. (1969) first black mayor in Mississippi since 1877: Charles _____
12. Many beautiful plantation mansions built before the _____ War are called "antebellum" houses.
13. The oldest town along the Mississippi R.
14. Vicksburg: the city where Coca-_____ was first bottled
16. Northern border state (abbr.)
18. State abbr.
19. Important dairy product

From States of Wonder published by GoodYearBooks. Copyright © 1992 Jeanne Cheyney and Arnold Cheyney.

# MISSISSIPPI

NAME _____     DATE _____

## MISSISSIPPI SUPPLY THE VOWEL

### DIRECTIONS

Look for the following words in the grid (the words not in parentheses). The words can go up, down, across, at angles, backward, or forward. Parts of words may overlap. Supply the correct vowel—*a e i o u*—for the center of each word group.

Pearl (river)
Pascagoula (the "singing river")
Tombigbee (river)
Mississippi (west-boundary river)
Yazoo (river)
(Big) Sun(flower) (river)
pine (important)
oak
magnolia (state tree)
cabbage
cowpea (vegetable)
cantaloupe
peach
watermelon
corn
cattle
bayou (slow-moving water)
Biloxi (chief port)

| C | B | O | H | K | N | C | I | P | A | G | J | A |
|---|---|---|---|---|---|---|---|---|---|---|---|---|
| C | ◯ | B | B | A | G | E | P | P | ◯ | A | R | L |
| K | L | T | T | F | O | K | P | R | P | A | G | D |
| E | U | I | T | O | Y | H | I | U | W | S | C | M |
| X | O | V | A | L | M | E | S | G | O | D | Z | H |
| C | G | H | J | M | E | B | S | P | C | B | T | L |
| O | A | R | U | X | A | S | ◯ | X | O | L | I | B |
| W | C | B | E | G | R | N | S | G | N | K | P | F |
| M | S | I | Q | D | E | U | S | T | B | T | H | V |
| L | A | J | M | Y | W | D | I | G | V | E | I | C |
| Z | P | G | W | A | T | N | M | Y | E | A | E | N |
| B | S | D | N | Z | R | K | C | J | O | W | P | A |
| F | A | S | N | ◯ | L | E | M | R | E | T | A | W |
| C | X | Y | C | O | L | T | Z | A | V | N | I | F |
| P | F | M | O | S | K | I | F | L | D | B | Z | O |
| G | R | E | P | ◯ | O | L | A | T | N | A | C | Q |
| B | Y | L | U | N | Y | B | C | L | Q | X | H | E |

mansion

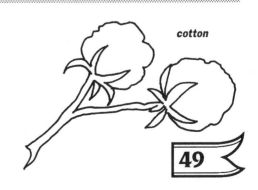

*cotton*

# MISSOURI

NAME _____ DATE _____

21. Southern wooded plateau
23. The first ice cream ____ were served in 1904.
24. Tallest U.S. monument: _____ Arch
27. St. Louis was once the ___ capital of the world.
28. An eastern border state (abbr.)
31. Mark _____, famous author of *Tom Sawyer*, was born in Missouri.
32. Farm animals: _____ cattle
33. An eastern border state (abbr.)
34. A western border state (abbr.)
35. Called "The ___ Me State"
36. Northern border state (abbr.)

## DOWN

2. The _____ River crosses from east to west.
5. Chief U.S. producer of _____ (a mineral)
10. Grazing livestock animals
14. Largest city: St. _____
16. A field crop: ____corn
18. Cartoonist Walt _____ lived in Missouri.
20. Capital: _____ City
22. A western border state (abbr.)
23. Name of a river
25. Independence: beginning of Santa Fe _____
26. Important fruit crop
29. An eastern border state (abbr.)
30. The bandit Jesse _____ was born in Missouri.

## MISSOURI CROSSWORD PUZZLE

### ACROSS

1. A tree: sweet _____
3. Southern border state (abbr.)
4. A tree
6. A field food crop
7. A famous black scientist who developed peanut products: George Washington _____
8. A precious metal
9. A field crop
11. A western border state (abbr.)
12. State tree: Flowering ___
13. Important field crop
15. Missouri is famous for raising horses and _____ (animals).
17. Independence: home of the 33rd U.S. President, Harry S. _____
19. The _____ River forms Missouri's eastern boundary

50

NAME _____     DATE _____

## MISSOURI
## CROSSING OVER

### DIRECTIONS

Use a pencil for this game. Find words from the following list that have the correct number of spaces and letters to fit into the crossing-over boxes (the words not in parentheses). Each word has a place where it belongs. The first word is done for you. To continue, find a 4-letter word with "e" in the second space, and so on. All the words tell about Missouri.

P E A C H E S

**3 letters**
fur (Indian trade)
hay
oak
(sweet) gum

**4 letters**
eggs
lead
coal
beef
milk
corn
hogs
oats
rice

*ice cream cone invented*

**5 letters**
(Mark) Twain (author)
sheep
wheat
Osage (river)
Black (river)
James (river)
(corncob) pipes (made)

**6 letters**
apples
Kansas (City)
silver
grapes
(jack) salmon
turkey

Current (river)
cypress
sorghum

**8 letters**
Columbia
bluebird (state bird)
Missouri (river)
hawthorn (state flower)
chickens
soybeans

**7 letters**
popcorn (crop)
tobacco
peaches

**9 letters**
(first) parachute (jump)

**10 letters**
watermelon
cottonwood (tree)

**12 letters**
Independence
kindergarten

*Gateway Arch*

**51**

# MONTANA

NAME _____    DATE _____

24. Montana is the ____-largest U.S. state.
25. Valuable logging tree: Douglas ____
29. Important irrigated crop
31. ____lands cover most of the state.
32. An eastern border state (abbr.)
33. A prairie-grazing farm animal

## DOWN
2. Western mountains
3. Called "The ____ State"
4. State abbr.
8. A leader in mining ____ (a metal)
9. A big game animal
13. A rugged national park
14. A U.S. leader in mining ____ (a metal)
18. A field crop
19. A U.S. leader in mining ____ (a metal)
21. Capital city
22. Lt. Col. George ____ and his troops fought the Indians at Little Big Horn and lost.
26. Western border state (abbr.)
27. Southern border state (abbr.)
28. A tree
30. An eastern border state (abbr.)

## MONTANA CROSSWORD PUZZLE

### ACROSS
1. Eureka: ____ tree capital of the world
5. Most towns have ____ with cowboys and cowgirls.
6. A river: ____head
7. An important irrigated crop: sugar ____
10. Northern border country
11. Largest city
12. Miles City has ____ horse contests.
15. Montana has the largest ____ deposits in the west (mineral).
16. Most valuable field crop
17. An early Indian tribe
20. State tree: Ponderosa ____
22. Most important farm animals
23. The most important liquid mineral

rodeos

From *States of Wonder* published by GoodYearBooks. Copyright © 1992 Jeanne Cheyney and Arnold Cheyney.

# MONTANA

NAME _____ DATE _____

## MONTANA NAME THE OUTLAW FIGHTERS

**DIRECTIONS**

Fill in the dotted lines with answers. If they are correct, the circled letters will tell who fought outlaws in the mining camps of Montana.

1. A small wild animal
2. Excellent logging tree: Douglas _____
3. A glacier named for the frozen insects that can still be seen in it
4. An important river
5. An important river
6. Big game animal (Pronghorn _____)
7. Natural product that insects make from nectar
8. State flower
9. Gideon _____ (Montana was the first to place them in hotel rooms to be read.)
10. Big game animal

1. _ _ _ ◯ _ _
2. _ ◯ _
3. ◯ _ _ _ _ _ _ _ _ _ _ _
4. _ ◯ _ _ _
5. _ _ _ ◯ _ _ _ _
6. _ _ ◯ _ _ _ _
7. _ _ ◯ _ _
8. _ _ _ ◯ _ _ _ _ _ _
9. _ _ _ ◯ _ _
10. _ _ _ ◯ _ _

## MONTANA SCRAMBLED WORDS

**DIRECTIONS**

Unscramble the words and write the answers on the lines provided. (Use scrap paper to work out your answers.)

1. The biggest fruit crop is **C B K L A   H R S I E E C R.** _____ _____

2. The state tree is **E P A N S O O R D   N I P E.** _____ _____

3. A grass that is good for grazing cattle is **U L A F B F O   S R G S A.** _____ _____

4. The name of a mountain Indian tribe is **E O S H O S H N.** _____

5. The name of a Plains Indian tribe is **T L E F K C B A E.** _____

6. A popular game bird in Montana is the **C D U K.** _____

7. A big game animal is the **E B R A.** _____

8. An important grazing livestock animal is the **P E S E H.** _____

*Christmas tree capital*

## MONTANA WORDS IN WORDS

How many words can you make from the letters in "Yellowstone," a national park with three entrances in Montana.

**YELLOWSTONE**

1. _____
2. _____
3. _____
4. _____
5. _____
6. _____
7. _____
8. _____
9. _____
10. _____

# NEBRASKA

NAME _____ DATE _____

27. National Historic Site: _____ Rock
30. 1922: largest mammoth _____ ever found (over 13 feet tall)
32. Most important farm animals: _____ cattle
33. _____ Park: rocks resemble toadstools
34. Many early farm settlers built homes from _____.

## DOWN

1. Near North Platte: home of _____ Bill
2. Northern border state (abbr.)
3. Priest and founder of Boy's Town: Edward _____
4. Indian tribe that hunted buffalo on the plains
7. State abbr.
10. The _____ Indians were farmers.
11. A tree
12. Rich _____ grasses are food for many cattle.
14. A tree
15. Much _____ for livestock is produced.
18. The _____ Trail ran from Omaha across the state.
19. _____ cover nearly all the state.
20. Great Sioux Indian chief: _____ Horse
23. North-central part of the state: huge _____
24. Nebraska has the largest planted _____ land in the U.S.
26. Western border state (abbr.)
28. Important farm animals
29. A southern border state (abbr.)
31. A southern border state (abbr.)

## NEBRASKA CROSSWORD PUZZLE

### ACROSS

5. Eastern border state (abbr.)
6. A wild flower: _____flower
8. Lewis and _____ explored eastern Nebraska.
9. Capital city
13. _____ Hills: hills covered with rich grass
16. A tree: _____ elder
17. Called "The _____ State"
19. 38th U.S. President born in Omaha: Gerald _____
21. The Indian word for Nebraska is Nebrathka, meaning "flat _____."
22. _____: a river and a tree
25. Largest city

54

# NEBRASKA

NAME _____     DATE _____

## NEBRASKA WORD SEARCHING

### DIRECTIONS

Find these hidden words in the grid (the words not in parentheses). They can go up, down, across, at an angle, forward, or backward.

(roller) skating (museum)
meadowlark (state bird)
Snake (river)
basswood (tree)
goldenrod (state flower)
cottonwood (state tree)
soybeans (important crop)
locust (tree)
sugar (beets)
corn (most important crop)
wheat (important crop)
bluestem (long prairie
    grass)
cedar
Platte (chief river)
Missouri (river, eastern
    border)
sorghum (grain)
sunflower
irrigated (much land)
feeders (farmers who fatten
    cattle)

| A | E | H | R | P | S | R | E | D | E | E | F | M |
|---|---|---|---|---|---|---|---|---|---|---|---|---|
| M | G | C | E | R | L | Q | D | S | N | A | K | E |
| X | S | O | Y | B | E | A | N | S | L | B | F | A |
| D | D | T | L | H | A | I | T | U | J | W | W | D |
| F | E | T | V | D | H | S | K | T | A | I | H | O |
| T | T | O | S | W | E | L | S | L | E | C | E | W |
| K | A | N | L | Z | C | N | H | W | K | Y | A | L |
| S | G | W | P | J | L | O | R | M | O | Z | T | A |
| R | I | O | B | T | X | J | H | O | M | O | B | R |
| E | R | O | L | A | V | T | R | N | D | I | D | K |
| W | R | D | U | S | U | G | A | R | V | R | O | F |
| O | I | W | E | T | N | P | D | M | S | U | D | E |
| L | N | J | S | I | U | Z | E | N | R | O | C | B |
| F | H | O | T | A | F | X | C | P | E | S | N | A |
| N | I | A | E | C | E | L | O | C | U | S | T | F |
| U | K | X | M | Y | D | C | I | L | P | I | G | Z |
| S | L | Q | T | S | O | R | G | H | U | M | W | K |

*sunflowers*

*buffalo*

55

# NEVADA

NAME _____   DATE _____

25. The U.S. tests _____ weapons in the desert.
26. A desert plant
27. A northern border state (abbr.)
28. Important ranch animals
29. Important ranch animals
32. A northern border state (abbr.)
33. Nevada has less _____ than any other state.
34. Largest city: Las _____

**DOWN**
2. Farmers water crops by _____.
4. Second largest city
5. An eastern border state (abbr.)
7. A tree
8. Hoover Dam created Lake _____, the largest man-made lake in the world.
10. Kit _____, frontiersman, was the guide for John Fremont.
11. Large wild animal: mule _____
13. The U.S. government owns over 85 percent of the _____.
17. The state permits _____.
20. A chief industry
21. Jedediah Smith lead _____ across the state.
22. Nevada once belonged to _____.
23. A desert plant
30. Western border state (abbr.)
31. Eastern border state (abbr.)

## NEVADA CROSSWORD PUZZLE

**ACROSS**
1. Rugged western mountain range: _____ Nevada
3. A dam on the Colorado River
6. Beautiful glacial lake
7. John _____ mapped Nevada in 1843.
9. State abbr.
12. Oldest permanent white settlement
14. A river
15. State has deep _____
16. Famous historic ghost town: _____ City
18. Comstock Lode: rich deposits of _____ and silver
19. Low spot in the Earth where water evaporates and leaves mud or a dry lake
24. Called "The _____ State"

# NEVADA

NAME _____ DATE _____

## NEVADA CLUE

### DIRECTIONS

Each set of lines has a vowel to help you determine the correct answer.

Desert plants:

__ a __ __ __ __ __

__ a __ __ __ __ __ __ __

__ __ __ __ a

Crops:

__ __ __ a __ __ __ __    __ __ __ __

__ a __

__ __ __ a __ __ __ __

__ __ __ a __

__ a __ __ __

Indian tribes:

__ __ e __ __ __

__ __ __ __ e

__ __ __ __ e

__ __ __ __ __ e

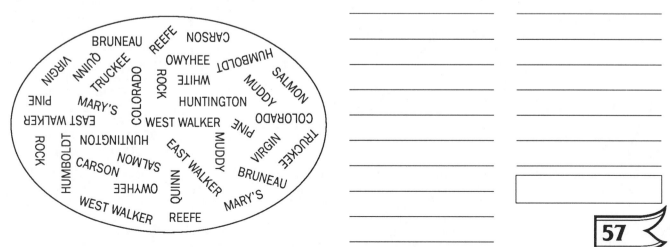

yucca

__ __ __ __ __ __ __ __ e

Wild animals:

__ o __ __ __ __

__ o __

__ __ __ __ o __

__ o __ __ __ __ __ __ __

__ __ __ o __ __ __    __ __ __ __ __

__ a __ __ __ __

__ __ __ __ __ __ a __

__ a __ __ __ __

__ __ a __ __ __

1. Valley of Fire State Park: strange __ o __ __ formations

2. Rhyolite: a ghost town with a building made from

   __ o __ __ __ __ __

## NEVADA RIVER AND CREEK PAIRS

### DIRECTIONS

All of the names of Nevada rivers and creeks in the center oval are in pairs, except one. Write the name of each river and creek pair on a blank. (Cross them off in the oval as you find them.) Then find the name that has no pair and write it in the box to the right.

BRUNEAU  REEFE  CARSON  VIRGIN  QUINN  TRUCKEE  OWYHEE  HUMBOLDT  ROCK  WHITE  SALMON  MUDDY  COLORADO  PINE  MARY'S  HUNTINGTON  EAST WALKER  WEST WALKER  PINE  VIRGIN  TRUCKEE  ROCK  HUMBOLDT  HUNTINGTON  CARSON  SALMON  EAST WALKER  NOWYEE  QUINN  MUDDY  BRUNEAU  MARY'S  WEST WALKER  REEFE

_____    _____

_____    _____

_____    _____

_____    _____

_____    _____

_____

_____

From *States of Wonder* published by GoodYearBooks. Copyright © 1992 Jeanne Cheyney and Arnold Cheyney.

NAME _____     DATE _____

24. Laconia: World's Sled-
    _____ Derby
25. Valuable tree
26. Leading dairy product
27. _____ cover 80 percent
    of the state
28. A forest product: maple
    _____
30. A poultry product
31. Famous poet: Robert
    _____

**DOWN**
 2. Beaches border the
    _____ ocean
 3. Southern border state
    (abbr.)
 8. Capital city
11. Important livestock
12. New Englanders are
    called _____.
14. New Hampshire Indian
    house
15. A game bird
17. State abbr.
18. Restored colonial
    seaport of the 1700s:
    _____ Banke
19. _____ tribe: enemy of
    New Hampshire Indians
20. A river
21. A field crop
22. Hillsboro: birthplace of
    14th U.S. President,
    Franklin _____
23. Large wild animal
29. Western border state
    (abbr.)

## NEW HAMPSHIRE CROSSWORD PUZZLE

**ACROSS**
 1. The highest peak: Mt.
    _____
 3. Eastern border state
    (abbr.)

 4. A fresh-water fish
 5. Most important field
    crop
 6. An early Indian tribe
 7. Largest city
 9. First U.S. _____
    shipbuilding yard:
    Portsmouth (1800)
10. Granite face on a

mountain: Great _____
Face
13. A tree
16. New Hampshire was
    the first of the original
    13 colonies to adopt its
    own _____.
21. Northern boundary
    country

58

From *States of Wonder* published by GoodYearBooks. Copyright © 1992 Jeanne Cheyney and Arnold Cheyney.

NAME _____   DATE _____

## NEW HAMPSHIRE NUMBER CODE

### DIRECTIONS

Look at the numbers under each line. Then find the matching number in the code box and write the letters on the answer lines.

| |
|---|
| A – 1 |
| B – 2 |
| C – 3 |
| D – 4 |
| E – 5 |
| F – 6 |
| G – 7 |
| H – 8 |
| I – 9 |
| J – 10 |
| K – 11 |
| L – 12 |
| M – 13 |
| N – 14 |
| O – 15 |
| P – 16 |
| Q – 17 |
| R – 18 |
| S – 19 |
| T – 20 |
| U – 21 |
| V – 22 |
| W – 23 |
| X – 24 |
| Y – 25 |
| Z – 26 |

**1. What happened in 1775?**

14 5 23   8 1 13 16 19 8 9 18 5   13 9 14 21 20 5 13 5 14

18 1 3 5 4   20 15   2 15 19 20 15 14 ' 13 1 ' 20 15   8 5 12 16

6 9 7 8 20   20 8 5   2 18 9 20 9 19 8 .

**2. What sports events happen in the White Mountains?**

19 11 9 9 14 7   3 15 13 16 5 20 9 20 9 15 14 19

**3. New Hampshire was the first to use something in 1947. What was it?**

1 18 20 9 6 9 3 9 1 12   18 1 9 14 :   19 3 9 5 14 20 9 19 20 19

21 19 5 4   4 18 25   9 3 5   20 15   " 19 5 5 4

3 12 15 21 4 19 "   1 14 4   3 1 21 19 5   18 1 9 14   15 22 5 18

1   6 15 18 5 19 20   6 9 18 5 .

**4. What is the most important agricultural activity?**

4 1 9 18 25   6 1 18 13 9 14 7

**5. Who were the early Indians? What did they do? Who was their enemy?**

20 8 5   1 12 7 15 14 17 21 9 1 14   9 14 4 9 1 14 19

6 1 18 13 5 4 '   8 21 14 20 5 4 '   6 9 19 8 5 4 '

1 14 4   2 21 9 12 20   23 9 7 23 1 13 19   15 6

2 1 18 11   1 14 4   19 11 9 14 19 .   20 8 5 9 18

5 14 5 13 25 :   9 18 15 17 21 15 9 19   9 14 4 9 1 14 19

*maple sugar*

NAME _____   DATE _____

## NEW JERSEY CROSSWORD PUZZLE

**ACROSS**
6. Early Indian tribe
10. Capital city
18. New Jersey: scene of many Revolutionary War _____
19. A hardwood tree
21. Many people _____ to New York City to work.
22. Important dairy product
23. Largest U.S. life insurance company (in Newark)
24. Most important vegetable crop
25. Electric light inventor from Menlo Park: Thomas _____
26. Large wild animal
27. A resort city: _____ Park
28. Western border state (abbr.)
29. State abbr.

**DOWN**
1. Largest city
2. Much of New Jersey's _____ produce goes to big eastern cities.
3. Western border state (abbr.)
4. First permanent European settlement (1660)
5. A tunnel connecting NJ and NY
6. First European settlers
7. Famous bridge from NJ to NY
8. A small water-loving wild animal
9. Another tunnel connecting NJ and NY
11. Coastal inlet: Great _____ Bay
12. Northern border state (abbr.)
13. Many people commute to work in _____ (Pennsylvania city).
14. First successful electric telegraph: Samuel F. B. _____
15. A river: _____stone
16. A tree: _____ pine
17. New Jersey is the most densely _____ state.
18. Important farm animals: _____ cattle
20. Called "The _____ State"

60

From *States of Wonder* published by GoodYearBooks. Copyright © 1992 Jeanne Cheyney and Arnold Cheyney.

# NEW JERSEY

NAME _____  DATE _____

## NEW JERSEY SUPPLY THE VOWEL

### DIRECTIONS

Look for the following words in the grid (the words not in parentheses). The words can go up, down, across, at angles, backward, or forward. Parts of words may overlap.  Supply the correct vowel—*a e i o u*—for the center of each word group.

cranberry (important crop)
hay
clams
Delaware (important river)
skunk
fruit (for eastern cities)
poultry (for eastern cities)
Hudson (river)
fox
oak
corn
tomato
peach
(1889) sewing (machine, electric)
vegetables (for eastern cities)
chemicals (important industry)
(Albert) Einstein (famous scientist)
Giants (Stadium)
(Woodrow) Wilson (U.S. President: 1912)
(Fort) Dix (army training)

| A | H | D | J | P | C | N | F | S | B | I | L | P |
| C | K | E | T | W | R | U | Q | S | K | H | O | D |
| V | R | L | Y | Z | X | G | M | F | R | O | I | T |
| C | L | O | M | S | G | E | C | A | L | D | N | O |
| E | H | W | N | Y | L | J | N | T | H | S | D | K |
| B | F | A | I | B | N | I | R | O | U | O | M | P |
| K | W | R | R | T | E | Y | Z | G | S | N | Q | V |
| O | V | E | A | D | G | R | N | B | Y | L | E | G |
| S | X | E | H | C | M | I | R | F | C | D | O | X |
| E | L | O | G | H | W | T | G | Y | Y | A | N | W |
| I | P | S | P | O | A | C | H | F | N | X | S | N |
| C | T | F | S | M | T | U | J | T | Q | C | T | R |
| K | O | A | K | I | D | A | S | N | S | K | E | B |
| X | M | R | O | C | W | E | B | G | C | V | I | M |
| V | A | J | N | A | D | K | W | L | I | F | N | R |
| P | T | U | I | L | A | H | B | S | E | B | X | A |
| J | O | Z | H | S | L | Z | E | Y | U | S | T | W |

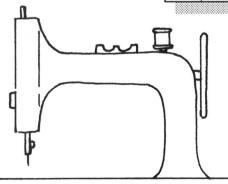

*sewing machine*

*snap beans*

61

NAME _____     DATE _____

24. Leading industry
26. Large wild animal: black
    ____
27. Mountain snow
    provides spring ____.
28. Western border state
    (abbr.)

**DOWN**
1. The first ____ bomb
   was built in 1945.
2. Western mountain
   range: ____ Mts.
6. Largest U.S. reserves
   of ____ (a fertilizer).
7. New Mexico has rocky,
   arid ____.
8. New Mexico has deep
   ____.
11. Capital city: ____ Fe
13. A tree
15. State tree
16. Early cattle thief and
    killer: Billy the ____
18. Research center for
    rockets and ____
    energy
19. Southern border
    country
20. Eastern border state
    (abbr.)
22. Largest national forest
25. State abbr.

## NEW MEXICO CROSSWORD PUZZLE

**ACROSS**
1. Largest city in NM
3. Important ranch
   animals
4. ____ falls throughout
   Arizona in winter.

5. A poisonous snake
7. ____ store water for
   irrigation.
9. Northern border state
   (abbr.)
10. Frontiersman and
    guide: Kit ____
12. Lake fish: black ____

14. Common tree
17. Former ruling country
19. New Mexico has rugged
    ____.
21. New Mexico is ____
    populated.
23. Important crop: chili
    ____ crop

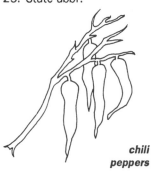

*chili
peppers*

From *States of Wonder* published by GoodYearBooks. Copyright © 1992 Jeanne Cheyney and Arnold Cheyney.

# NEW MEXICO

NAME _____ DATE _____

## NEW MEXICO NAME THE FAMOUS NATIONAL PARK

**DIRECTIONS**

Fill in the dotted lines with answers. If they are correct, the circled letters will spell the name of a famous New Mexico national park.

1. Important vegetable crop
2. A poisonous snake
3. Fierce, famous Apache Indian warrior
4. Important dairy product
5. Desert plant
6. Important farm animals
7. State flower
8. State bird

9. New Mexico is called the Land of _____.
10. Ancient Indians, about 700 A.D., who built many-storied houses
11. Mexican bandit
12. Indian tribe living in apartment-like stone (or adobe) dwellings
13. River running the length of the state
14. Famous mission (1610)
15. A river

## NEW MEXICO ALPHABET SEARCH

**DIRECTIONS**

Find at least four names of New Mexico game birds, trees, rivers, and wild animals that have letters of the alphabet used only once in each *individual* word. Example: black bear (yes, because the letters are used only once in each individual word).

Game Birds _____

_____   _____

Trees   _____

_____

_____   Wild Animals

_____

_____   _____

**Pronghorn antelope**

Rivers   _____

_____

_____

63

# NEW YORK

NAME _____    DATE _____

31. State's leading dairy product
32. A fruit crop
33. Leads all states in _____ trade
34. State abbr.
35. A Long Island coastal catch: striped _____

## DOWN

1. An eastern border state (abbr.)
2. A field crop: _____ crop
3. New York City: one of the world's biggest, busiest _____
4. Manhattan's famous park
5. A fruit crop: _____ crop
7. Leading U.S. _____ center
8. Headquarters for the United _____
13. Busiest international airport in the U.S.
14. An eastern border state (abbr.)
15. A field crop
16. A night-flying bird
17. Capital city
18. World-famous mountain resort: Lake _____
20. Important tree: _____ maple
23. A Great Lake bordering New York state
24. An early explorer: Henry _____
26. A leading fruit crop
27. World's largest indoor theater: _____ City Music Hall
28. A leading field crop
29. A poultry product
30. A leading field crop

## NEW YORK CROSSWORD PUZZLE

### ACROSS

6. An eastern border state (abbr.)
7. A vegetable crop: snap _____ crop
9. _____ was once New Amsterdam.
10. A southern border state (abbr.)
11. New York: named for the _____ of York
12. Largest city in the U.S.: New _____
19. A southern border state (abbr.)
21. A Lake Erie and Lake Ontario fish
22. Symbol of freedom: Statue of _____
25. State's natural wonder: _____ Falls

From *States of Wonder* published by GoodYearBooks. Copyright © 1992 Jeanne Cheyney and Arnold Cheyney.

# NEW YORK

NAME _____ DATE _____

## NEW YORK CROSSING OVER

### DIRECTIONS
Use a pencil for this game. Find words from the following list that have the correct number of spaces and letters to fit into the crossing-over boxes (the words not in parentheses). Each word has a place where it belongs. The first word is done for you. To continue, find a seven-letter word with "p" in the third space, and so on. All the words tell about New York.

3 letters
owl
eel (fish)
(Uncle) Sam
oak
hay
4 letters
(Duke of) York
(Hyde) Park
Duke (of York)
milk
eggs
rose (state flower)
work
5 letters
(former governor) Dewey
Radio (City Music Hall)
(West) Point (military
   academy)
sheep
maple
skunk
6 letters
Finger (Lakes)
(called) Empire (State)
Hudson (river)
Mohawk (river)
cattle
potato
oyster
spruce
7 letters
clothes (center for)
(first) capital
   (New York City)
Buffalo (port)
Central (Park)
(Lake) Ontario
forests (cover
   half of NY)
Kennedy (airport)
foreign (trade leader)
poultry
lobster
seaport

APPALACHIAN

**Statue of Liberty**

8 letters
Catskill (Mts.)
Iroquois (Indians)
(President) McKinley
   (shot in Buffalo)

cultural (center)
bluebird (state bird)
flounder (fish)
9 letters
(New) Amsterdam

10 letters
Algonquian (Indians)
publishing (center for)
11 letters
Appalachian (Mts.)

65

# NORTH CAROLINA

NAME _____    DATE _____

21. Largest city
25. Northern border state (abbr.)
28. _____ cover two-thirds of NC.
30. A tree
31. State abbr.

**DOWN**
1. The Lost Colony: _____ Island (1587)
3. Blue _____ Mountains
6. Protesters: Sons of _____
13. A southern border state (abbr.)
15. Western North Carolina has high _____.
18. Island hideout of pirate Blackbeard
19. Restored colonial village: Old _____
20. Revolutionary War: first state to vote for _____
22. A river
23. Called "The _____ Heel State"
24. Furniture capital of U.S.: High _____
26. A river
27. Large wild animal
29. A southern border state (abbr.)

## NORTH CAROLINA CROSSWORD PUZZLE

**ACROSS**
1. Capital city
2. Swiss and German town: New _____ (1710)
4. Greensboro: largest _____ mills
5. Kitty Hawk: first _____ flight
7. Western border state (abbr.)
8. North Carolina shore: very dangerous to _____
9. A poultry product
10. Important field crop
11. NC is a leader in raising _____ potatoes.
12. Large river: Cape _____
14. A U.S. leader in raising _____ (poultry)
16. An important field crop
17. A lake and river fish

*furniture*

From States of Wonder published by GoodYearBooks. Copyright © 1992 Jeanne Cheyney and Arnold Cheyney.

# NORTH CAROLINA

From *States of Wonder* published by GoodYearBooks. Copyright © 1992 Jeanne Cheyney and Arnold Cheyney.

NAME _____ DATE _____

## NORTH CAROLINA CLUE

### DIRECTIONS
Each set of lines has a vowel to help you determine the correct answer.

1. Highest mountain peak: Mt. _____

   1. __ i __ __ __ __ __ __

2. Tourist attraction estate near Asheville

   2. __ i __ __ __ __ __ __

3. A forest tree

   3. __ i __ __ __ __

4. Early coastal Indians

   4. __ u __ __ __ __ __ __ __

5. U.S. leader in this wood industry

   5. __ u __ __ __ __ __ __

6. Farm poultry

   6. __ u __ __ __

7. Party loyal to the English King (1775)

   7. __ __ __ i __ __

8. Party opposing the English King (1775)

   8. __ __ i __ __

9. Leads U.S. and many nations in this industry

   9. __ __ __ __ i __ __

10. Valuable food crop

   10. __ __ a __ __ __ __

11. Early coastal and Piedmont Indians

   11. __ a __ __ __ __ __

12. First North Carolina town (1705)

   12. __ a __ __

13. Valuable fishing catch

   13. __ __ a __ __

14. Eastern part of the state is called the _____ region

   14. __ o __ __ __ __ __

15. Western mountain Indian reservation

   15. __ __ __ __ o __ __ __

16. Large river in western NC: French _____

   16. __ __ o __ __

17. Name of the central region of NC

   17. __ __ __ __ __ o __ __

18. Valuable farm animals

   18. __ o __ __

19. Restored governor's palace in New Bern

   19. __ __ __ o __

20. Valuable field crop

   20. __ __ __ __ e __ __

21. Most important poultry (5 to 12 weeks old)

   21. __ __ __ __ __ e __ __

## NORTH CAROLINA WORDS IN WORDS

How many words can you make from the letters in "Petersburg Railroad," the first interstate railroad that was opened between two states in 1833?

**PETERSBURG RAILROAD**

1. _____
2. _____
3. _____
4. _____
5. _____
6. _____
7. _____
8. _____
9. _____
10. _____
11. _____
12. _____
13. _____
14. _____

*bear*

67

NAME _____    DATE _____

17. Huge wheat farms:
    _____ River Valley
20. Wild fruit: wild _____
21. Largest city
22. Important field crop
25. Northern border country
29. State tree: American
    _____
30. Western border state
    (abbr.)

**DOWN**
1. Leading U.S. producer:
   _____ seeds
2. Eastern tree
4. Eastern border state
   (abbr.)
5. Most valuable farm
   animals: dairy _____
10. Called "The _____ State"
11. Important field crop:
    _____ beets
14. Valley of weird
    formations
16. Burning coal beds turn
    clay peaks above them
    into bright red and pink
    _____.
18. Explorers Lewis and
    Clark built Fort _____.
19. State abbr.
23. Important field crop
24. Chief field crop (grown
    in every county)
25. Has enormous reserves
    of _____ (mineral)
26. Dog towns are formed
    by prairie _____.
27. Important field crop
28. Eastern border state
    (abbr.)

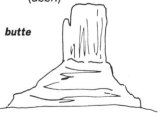

*butte*

## NORTH DAKOTA CROSSWORD PUZZLE

**ACROSS**
1. A nickname for North
   Dakota: "_____ State"
3. Garrison _____ produces
   electric power.
5. Early Indian tribe

6. U.S. leader in growing
   _____ (field crop)
7. A tree growing in the
   Myrtle Mts.
8. Steep hills that stand
   alone
9. Important dairy product
10. North Dakota is mainly
    a _____ state.

12. Most valuable liquid
    mineral
13. Important vegetable
    crop: _____ beans
14. Capital city
15. A tree known for its
    trembling leaves
16. Southern border state
    (abbr.)

# NORTH DAKOTA

NAME _____ DATE _____

## NORTH DAKOTA WORD SEARCHING

### DIRECTIONS

Find these hidden North Dakota words in the grid (the words not in parentheses). They can go up, down, across, at an angle, backward, or forward.

Rivers:
    Missouri
    James
    Knife
(Lake) Sakakawea (formed by a dam)
combine (machine for harvesting wheat)
Rugby (approximate geographic center of North America)
(Dakota means): friends
squirrel (Flickertail)
escarpment (steep slope)
roads (scoria is used to resurface them)
Garrison (large dam)
Crops:
    flaxseed (half of the U.S. crop)
    durum (wheat used to make spaghetti and macaroni)
    barley
    sunflower (seeds: top U.S. supplier)
Farm products:
    hogs
    milk
Myrtle (Mts.)
prairie (dogs)
bonanza (large profit made on farms)

| B | F | J | I | Y | A | E | I | R | I | A | R | P |
|---|---|---|---|---|---|---|---|---|---|---|---|---|
| Y | M | E | B | O | N | A | N | Z | A | C | K | G |
| E | S | G | E | D | O | B | T | N | H | S | K | S |
| L | U | A | S | M | E | S | I | R | T | L | P | L |
| R | N | O | C | F | C | Q | Y | D | I | F | Q | T |
| A | F | J | A | L | R | U | F | M | J | G | B | C |
| B | L | B | R | T | W | I | U | F | Z | A | D | O |
| Q | O | M | P | H | F | R | E | D | U | R | U | M |
| S | W | H | M | F | K | R | S | N | S | R | E | B |
| A | E | D | E | M | B | E | J | E | D | I | A | I |
| K | R | E | N | R | E | L | L | G | M | S | L | N |
| A | U | E | T | P | C | T | O | K | R | O | H | E |
| K | G | S | A | L | R | D | B | J | S | N | P | T |
| A | L | X | K | Y | A | R | O | A | D | S | Y | S |
| W | M | A | M | V | Q | S | T | M | W | A | N | G |
| E | W | L | U | K | N | I | F | E | B | D | C | O |
| A | C | F | I | R | U | O | S | S | I | M | U | H |

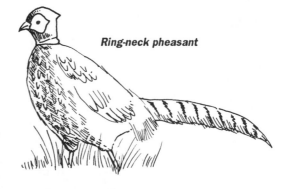

*Ring-neck pheasant*

# OHIO

NAME _____    DATE _____

23. U.S. leader in producing _____ stone
24. Wild flower: wild _____
25. Very important mined mineral
27. Large wild animal
28. Astronaut born in Ohio: John _____
29. Important poultry product
30. Important fruit crop
31. Most of Ohio's people live in the _____ east.
32. 27th U.S. president, born in Ohio
33. A leading producer of _____ (animal product)
36. Important field crop: _____ crop

## DOWN

1. A river
2. Southern border state (abbr.)
3. Called "The _____ State"
4. Dayton: C.F. Kettering developed self-starter for _____
6. The Underground Railroad helped _____.
12. Hardwood tree
14. Capital city
16. Lake and stream fish: _____ fish
17. Seven _____ were born in Ohio.
19. An eastern border state (abbr.)
20. Indian mound: Great _____ Mound
26. Orville and Wilbur Wright made _____ flights.
34. State abbr.
35. An eastern border state (abbr.)

## OHIO CROSSWORD PUZZLE

### ACROSS

5. Cincinnati _____: first pro baseball team
7. Field crop
8. Leading U.S. producer: _____ (mineral)
9. Chief field crop
10. Northern border state (abbr.)
11. Leading dairy product
13. Northern border lake
14. Tuscarawas County: called "Little Switzerland" for its _____
15. A leading U.S. state for raising _____ (farm animals)
16. Largest city
18. Lake and stream fish: _____gill
21. Canton: Pro Football Hall of _____
22. Leading state for _____ products

70

From *States of Wonder* published by GoodYearBooks. Copyright © 1992 Jeanne Cheyney and Arnold Cheyney.

# O H I O

NAME _____ DATE _____

## OHIO RIVER PAIRS

### DIRECTIONS

All of the Ohio river names in the center oval are in pairs, except one. Write the name of each river pair on a blank. (Cross them off in the oval as you find them.) Then find the name of the river that has no pair and write it in the box.

_____          _____

_____          _____

_____          _____

_____          _____

_____          _____

_____          _____

_____   _____   _____   _____

(River names in oval: ST. MARY, BLANCHARD, HOCKING, MOHICAN, WABASH, HURON, CUYAHOGA, KOKOSING, ST. JOSEPH, AUGLAIZE, TIFFIN, SANDUSKY, PORTAGE, VERMILLION, MAUMEE, GRAND, MUSKINGUM, BLANCHARD, ST. MARY, MUSKINGUM, OLENTANGY, SCIOTO, MAUMEE, GRAND, OHIO, AUGLAIZE, ST. JOSEPH, WALHONDING, HOCKING, WABASH, TIFFIN, OHIO, OLENTANGY, MIAMI, KOKOSING, PORTAGE, SCIOTO, LICKING, CUYAHOGA, WALHONDING, HURON, MIAMI, VERMILLION, MOHICAN)

## OHIO SKYSCRAPER

### DIRECTIONS

Write your answers in the boxes. The circled letters will help you.

1. State abbr.
2. Medium-size wild animal
3. Farm crop: pop_____
4. Barberton: first _____ books
5. A vegetable crop
6. Cleveland: first electric _____ lights
7. Author of famous beginning readers in the 1800s
8. Astronaut born in Ohio: Neil A. _____
9. Large eastern city
10. Eastern Ohio: _____ Plateau
11. Eastern border state

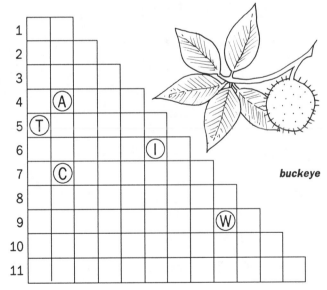

(Grid rows numbered 1–11; circled letters: A in row 4, T in row 5, I in row 6, C in row 7, W in row 9)

*buckeye*

## OHIO WORDS IN WORDS

How many words can you make from the letters in "Underground Railroad," a route that helped southern slaves escape to Canada?

### UNDERGROUND RAILROAD

1. _____   4. _____   7. _____   10. _____

2. _____   5. _____   8. _____

3. _____   6. _____   9. _____

# OKLAHOMA

**DOWN**

1. Important field crop: _____ beans
2. Tsa-La-Gi: _____ Indian village
3. Small forest animal: _____ (famous for its fur)
4. Near Tahlequah: "Trail of _____" drama
5. A city
6. Choctaw Indian words: *okla* means "_____" and *homma* means "red"
7. Cattle: fattened for market in _____ lots
8. Lake and stream fish: _____ fish
9. Leading agricultural income: _____ cattle
11. Oklahoma has over 5 _____ beef cattle.
12. Oklahoma City: National _____ Hall of Fame
14. Has vast _____ reserves (liquid mineral)
15. An eastern border state (abbr.)
16. Fort _____ was established in 1869.
17. Has rich beds of _____ (mineral)
20. A western border state (abbr.)
21. The _____ Bowl forced farmers to leave OK in the 1930s.
23. An eastern border state (abbr.)
24. _____ harvest wheat.
25. Most valuable field crop
26. Important field crop
27. Called "The _____ State"
34. Southwestern border state (abbr.)

## OKLAHOMA CROSSWORD PUZZLE

**ACROSS**

1. Oklahoma has more than _____ Indian tribes.
2. A northern border state (abbr.)
10. An Indian tribe
11. First automatic parking _____ (1935)
13. Tulsa: International _____ Final
18. State abbr.
22. Capital and largest city: _____ City
28. Oklahoma City:

National _____ Hall of Fame
29. Important farm animals
30. Oklahoma: center of _____ culture
31. A wild flower
32. An important tree
33. An Indian tribe
35. Important poultry

From *States of Wonder* published by GoodYearBooks. Copyright © 1992 Jeanne Cheyney and Arnold Cheyney.

# OKLAHOMA

NAME _____   DATE _____

## OKLAHOMA SCRAMBLED WORDS

### DIRECTIONS
Unscramble the words and write the answers on the lines provided. (Use scrap paper to work out your answers.)

1. Two prairie plants are **I E Q E T U S M** and **H G R S S U E A B**. _____   _____

2. Two great rivers are the **E R D** and **S R N A A A K S**. _____   _____

3. Two important livestock products are **G S E G** and **L M K I**. _____   _____

4. Two important farm crops are **E U S T N P A** and **Y A H**. _____   _____

5. Two important trees are **O I Y C H R K** and **T A N L W U**. _____   _____

6. The early Plains Indians followed the **L U A F O B F   R D H E S**. _____

## OKLAHOMA SAME FIRST LETTER

### DIRECTIONS
The circled letter is the first letter for each answer. Example:

(**P**)
— i — e —
DESSERT
u  p  p  y
YOUNG DOG

(**O**)
_ _ _ _ _ _ _ _
MOUNTAINS
_ _ _ _ _ _ _
SMALL WILD ANIMAL

(**W**)
_ _ _ _ _ _ _ _ _
MOUNTAINS
_ _ _   _ _ _ _ _ _
WILD FLOWER

(**A**)
_ _ _ _ _ _ _
PLAINS ANIMAL
_ _ _ _ _ _ _ _ _
MOUNTAINS

(**C**)
_ _ _ _ _ _
IMPORTANT CROP
_ _ _ _ _ _ _
IMPORTANT POULTRY

(**P**)
_ _ _ _ _ _
A RIVER
_ _ _ _ _ _   _ _ _
SMALL PLAINS ANIMAL

(**C**)
_ _ _ _ _ _ _ _ _
A RIVER
_ _ _ _ _ _ _
A RIVER

(**C**)
_ _ _ _ _ _ _ _
INDIAN TRIBE
_ _ _ _ _ _ _ _
FAMOUS OLD CATTLE TRAIL

(**S**)
_ _ _ _ _ _ _ _
CITY
_ _ _ _ _ _ _
FIELD CROP

(**T**)
_ _ _ _ _ _
CITY
_ _ _ _ _ _
POULTRY

*rodeo*

NAME _____    DATE _____

22. Forest owners plant trees on tree _____.
24. A southern border state (abbr.)
26. A softwood tree
28. World's largest forest of lava-cast _____
29. A leading fruit crop: _____ crop
30. Portland's nickname: City of _____
32. A hardwood tree
33. Deepest lake in the U.S.: _____ Lake

**DOWN**
1. Some coastline has sandy _____.
2. An eastern border state (abbr.)
4. A leading field crop
6. Important farm animals
7. Leads the U.S. in growing _____ (nuts)
9. A mighty river
11. Leads the U.S. in producing peppermint _____
12. A southern border state (abbr.)
14. John _____ River
16. Astoria: first _____ fur-trading post
18. Steep _____ rise along much of the coast.
19. Irrigation is needed for the _____ crop.
20. Northern border state (abbr.)
23. A river
25. Important farm animals: _____ cattle
27. _____ lion caves are on the Pacific coast.

## OREGON CROSSWORD PUZZLE

**ACROSS**
1. Famous Columbia River dam
3. Most valuable crop
5. Called "The _____ State"
8. Coastal fish: _____fish
10. State tree: Douglas _____
11. Covered wagons traveled on the _____ Trail.
13. Capital city
15. U.S. leader in _____ production (forest product)
16. Melted mountain snow and rain provide pure _____.
17. Important field crop: sugar _____
19. Largest city
21. Highest mountain peak: Mount _____

From *States of Wonder* published by GoodYearBooks. Copyright © 1992 Jeanne Cheyney and Arnold Cheyney.

# OREGON

NAME _____ DATE _____

## OREGON SUPPLY THE VOWEL

### DIRECTIONS

Look for the following words in the grid (the words not in parentheses). The words can go up, down, across, at angles, backward, or forward. Parts of words may overlap. Supply the correct vowel—*a e i o u*—for the center of each word group.

(largest producer of peppermint) oil
(famous canyon) Hells
evergreen (vast forest)
berries
salmon
cod
Columbia
plum
potato (chief vegetable crop)
irrigation
barley
forest (area: covers half of OR)
(sea lion) caves
(1792: Captain) Gray (named the Columbia River for his ship)
Wallowa (scenic mountains)
milk
Pacific
(flower) bulb (important industry)
crab

| A | C | H | G | I | B | E | N | L | J | S | A | O |
|---|---|---|---|---|---|---|---|---|---|---|---|---|
| G | W | T | Y | C | Q | U | C | P | N | H | I | V |
| P | R | W | R | T | S | E | R | ◯ | F | T | B | S |
| X | C | ◯ | V | E | S | G | M | T | D | A | M | B |
| H | B | L | Y | O | V | L | I | A | P | L | ◯ | M |
| E | Q | L | P | M | A | E | Y | T | C | L | L | B |
| A | K | O | U | S | D | T | R | O | B | D | O | S |
| J | O | W | M | I | C | S | P | G | N | P | C | K |
| L | R | A | T | R | L | A | C | U | R | B | H | B |
| Y | F | D | O | R | C | B | A | R | L | ◯ | Y | I |
| H | P | Z | M | ◯ | L | K | Q | B | L | R | E | A |
| O | K | T | F | G | L | W | R | L | A | R | G | N |
| S | Q | I | B | A | N | H | S | W | E | I | A | U |
| O | C | P | X | T | M | J | R | D | B | E | L | N |
| Y | U | M | Z | I | Y | P | Z | V | M | S | D | E |
| A | K | T | Q | O | X | H | V | J | W | F | O | I |
| L | S | E | R | N | S | F | B | G | N | T | C | N |

beaver

sea lion

seal

# PENNSYLVANIA

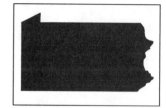

23. A southern border state (abbr.)
24. Prized game animal: black _____
25. The Declaration of Independence was signed at _____ Hall.
29. World's largest chocolate factory
30. Pennsylvania _____ people are known for fine cooking and colorful designs on buildings.
31. Historic National Military Park

**DOWN**
2. Valuable dairy product
5. Major industry: _____making
6. Supplies all the _____ coal in the U.S.
8. Eastern boundary river
9. Philadelphia was the nation's first _____ city.
12. Pittsburgh is on the _____ River.
14. Northern boundary lake
16. Valuable dairy animals
17. A southern border state (abbr.)
20. State abbr.
21. Philadelphia: home of the _____ Bell
26. An eastern border state (abbr.)
27. A leading field crop
28. A leading U.S. poultry product

## PENNSYLVANIA CROSSWORD PUZZLE

**ACROSS**
1. Northeastern border state (abbr.)
3. A southern border state (abbr.)
4. Pennsylvania is one of the nation's most _____ states.
7. The ice cream _____ was invented (Philadelphia, 1874).
10. Valuable farm animals: _____ cattle
11. The King of England gave Pennsylvania to William _____.
13. Largest city
15. Lake fish
18. National forest
19. A leading fruit crop
21. President _____ gave the Gettysburg Address.
22. Capital city

*Hershey chocolate*

From *States of Wonder* published by GoodYearBooks. Copyright © 1992 Jeanne Cheyney and Arnold Cheyney.

# PENNSYLVANIA

NAME _____     DATE _____

## PENNSYLVANIA NAME THE MOUNTAIN RANGE

**DIRECTIONS**
Fill in the dotted lines with answers. If they are correct, the circled letters will spell the name of a Pennsylvania mountain range.

1. The _____ travel in horse-drawn carriages and use no electricity.
2. Pennsylvania means _____ _____.
3. Philadelphia: Mummers _____ (January 1st.)
4. A mountain range and river
5. Location of one of the world's largest stone-arched bridges
6. A leading field crop
7. Beautiful mountains with spectacular waterfalls
8. Pennsylvania leads the U.S. in growing _____, a greenhouse crop that needs dampness.
9. Gettysburg: U.S. President Abraham _____ gave a famous speech to dedicate part of the battlefield as a cemetery
10. Important fruit crop
11. Pennsylvania is called "The _____ State."

1. ◯ _ _ _ _
2. ◯ _ _ _ ' _  _ _ _ _ _
3. ◯ _ _ _ _ _
4. ◯ _ _ _ _ _
5. _ _ _ _ _ ◯ _ _
6. _ ◯ _
7. _ _ _ ◯ _ _
8. _ _ _ ◯ _ _ _
9. _ ◯ _ _
10. ◯ _ _ _ _
11. _ _ _ _ _ ◯ _

*Amish*

## PENNSYLVANIA SAME FIRST LETTER

**DIRECTIONS**
The circled letter is the first letter for each answer. Example:

◯P   i_ _e
     DESSERT
     u _ p _p _ y
     YOUNG DOG

◯A   _ _ _ _ _
     FRUIT
     _ _ _ _ _ _ _ _ _
     INDIANS

◯Q   AMISH ARE KNOWN AS _____ PEOPLE.
     _ _ _ _ _ _
     WILLIAM PENN WAS A _____.

◯S   _ _ _ _ _ _ _ _ _
     LARGE RIVER
     _ _ _ _ _ _
     FIRST PERMANENT SETTLERS WERE FROM _____.

◯P   _ _ _ _ _ _
     FRUIT
     _ _ _ _ _ _ _ _ _ _ _
     A CITY

◯G   _ _ _ _ _ _ _ _
     A LEADING U.S. INDUSTRY
     _ _ _ _ _ _
     STATE BIRD: RUFFED

◯P   _ _ _ _ _ _ _ _ _
     MANUFACTURING CITY
     _ _ _ _ _ _
     A BEAUTIFUL CANYON: _____ _____ GORGE

NAME _____    DATE _____

18. Rhode Island has no _____.
19. A poultry product
20. Rhode _____ includes 36 islands.
25. Large wild animal
26. In size, Rhode Island is the _____ U.S. state.
27. Capital and largest city
28. Western border state (abbr.)

## DOWN
2. South-boundary ocean
4. State abbr.
6. _____ Bay nearly cuts RI in two.
10. Coastal fish: _____fish
13. A common bird
15. A night-flying bird: barred _____
16. Famous _____: Rhode Island Reds
17. Newport coastal waters: _____ Races
19. A forest tree
21. Pawtucket: historic _____ Mill
22. State flower
23. A lake and river fish
24. Rhode Island formerly had many coastal _____yards.

## RHODE ISLAND CROSSWORD PUZZLE

### ACROSS
1. Northeastern border state (abbr.)
3. Lake and river fish
5. First water-powered cotton-_____ mill (1700s)
7. A leading resort center: _____ Island
8. A leading field crop
9. Newport: The _____, one of many huge mansions
11. New England's longest suspension bridge
12. Small, water-loving wild animal
14. Narraganset _____: peaceful people who hunted, fished, and farmed
15. Called "The _____ State"

*yacht races*

NAME _____  DATE _____

## RHODE ISLAND MORSE CODE

### DIRECTIONS

Look at the dots and dashes under each line. Then find the matching dots and dashes in the code box and write the code letters on the answer lines.

| | |
|---|---|
| A | ._ |
| B | _... |
| C | _._. |
| D | _.. |
| E | . |
| F | .._. |
| G | __. |
| H | .... |
| I | .. |
| J | .___ |
| K | _._ |
| L | ._.. |
| M | __ |
| N | _. |
| O | ___ |
| P | .__. |
| Q | __._ |
| R | ._. |
| S | ... |
| T | _ |
| U | .._ |
| V | ..._ |
| W | .__ |
| X | _.._ |
| Y | _.__ |
| Z | __.. |

1. What was built in 1763?

2. What is an important Rhode Island industry?

3. What is Rhode Island famous for? Why?

*swordfish*

*Rhode Island
Red chicken*

4. What was built in Newport in 1892?

NAME _____

DATE _____

27. Important field crop

## DOWN

2. An important industry: _____ (cloth)
3. The eastern part of South Carolina is called the _____ country.
5. Large, beautiful homes with much farmland
8. Important farm animals: _____ cattle
10. First battle of the Civil War: Fort _____
11. _____ cover nearly two-thirds of South Carolina.
12. Capital and largest city
13. Leading farm crop
14. A leading resort area: _____ Head Island
15. State bird: Carolina _____
16. A field crop
17. An important fruit crop
19. A Revolutionary War victory: Battle of _____
20. Permanent English settlement (1680): _____ Towne
23. Important field crop

## SOUTH CAROLINA CROSSWORD PUZZLE

### ACROSS

1. Eastern boundary ocean
4. The western part of South Carolina is called _____ country.
6. Mountains: _____ Ridge
7. River on southwestern border
9. Revolutionary War: Battle of _____ Mountain
11. First _____proof building (1826)
17. Called "The _____ State"
18. State abbr.
21. Western border state (abbr.)
22. A rolling upland
24. Important coastal fishing catch
25. Northeastern border state (abbr.)
26. Forestry farmers sell _____.

*Blackbeard*

From *States of Wonder* published by GoodYearBooks. Copyright © 1992 Jeanne Cheyney and Arnold Cheyney.

NAME _____   DATE _____

## SOUTH CAROLINA CROSSING OVER

### DIRECTIONS

Use a pencil for this game. Find words from the following list that have the correct number of spaces and letters to fit into the crossing-over boxes (the words not in parentheses). Each word has a place where it belongs. The first word is done for you. To continue, find a 7-letter word with "k" in the fourth space, and so on. All the words tell about South Carolina.

**3 letters**
- hay
- (Pee) Dee (river)
- fox
- (wild) cat

**4 letters**
- (black) bear
- pine
- corn
- milk
- (Spanish) moss
- hogs
- oats
- eggs (most valuable poultry product)
- (Carolina) wren (state bird)
- lime (stone)
- part (of NC is called Low Country)

**5 letters**
- wheat
- Broad (river)
- (Wateree) river
- yucca (plant)
- Kings (Mt. battle)
- clams
- crabs
- shark
- birds (over 450 kinds)

**6 letters**
- timber
- Ashley (river)
- Santee (river)
- (Fort) Sumter

- Parris (Island: Marine training base)
- apples
- cattle
- cotton
- (Francis) Marion (known as the Swamp Fox)
- oyster (beds)
- azalea (flowering shrub)
- (30) Indian (tribes)

**7 letters**
- peaches (important crop)
- turkeys
- granite
- nursery (plants)

- peanuts
- Catawba (Indians)
- tobacco
- (Venus) flytrap (plant)
- (Sumner) nuclear (power plant)

**8 letters**
- Combahee (river)
- Cherokee (Indians)
- broilers (young chickens)
- Beaufort (historic town)
- tomatoes
- potatoes
- Palmetto (state tree)

- Savannah (river)

**9 letters**
- Albemarle

**10 letters**
- Charleston (historic city)
- Blackbeard (fierce pirate)
- greenhouse (plants)
- alligators

**11 letters**
- watermelons

**BLACKBEARD**

From *States of Wonder* published by GoodYearBooks. Copyright © 1992 Jeanne Cheyney and Arnold Cheyney.

81

NAME _____     DATE _____

27. Famous Indian chief:
    _____ Bull
28. Northern border state
    (abbr.)
29. Important grazing
    animal
31. State abbr.
32. U.S. leader in raising
    _____ (poultry)

**DOWN**
 2. Largest city: _____ Falls
 3. Black Hills: granite
    statue of Sioux Chief
    _____ Horse
 4. The _____ River flows
    through the middle of
    the state.
 6. An isolated hill with a
    flat top and steep sides
 8. Eastern border state
    (abbr.)
 9. A river fish: Rainbow
    _____
12. Homestake Mine: one
    of the Western
    Hemisphere's greatest
    _____ mines.
15. Steamboat on the Miss-
    issippi River (1831)
16. Battle of _____ Knee
    (1890)
17. A leading field crop
18. Ranchers called _____
    fatten young cattle.
20. Weirdly beautiful area:
    _____ National Park
22. Important grazing
    animals
25. Important dairy product
26. A wild flower
30. Eastern border state
    (abbr.)

## SOUTH DAKOTA CROSSWORD PUZZLE

**ACROSS**
 1. Famous national
    memorial: Mt. _____
 5. Capital city
 7. Famous frontiersman
    and marshall: Wild Bill
    _____
 8. Important industry:
    _____ packing
10. State tree: Black Hills
    _____
11. A tree
13. A leader in producing
    sheep's _____
14. Western border state
    (abbr.)
19. Lawless gold-mining
    town (1826):
21. Large wild animal
23. Sioux, or _____, Indians
    followed buffalo herds.
24. A leading field crop

# SOUTH DAKOTA

NAME _____    DATE _____

## SOUTH DAKOTA CLUE

### DIRECTIONS
Each set of lines has a vowel to help you determine the correct answer.

1. Mitchell: famous Corn _____

2. State flower: American

3. State bird: ring-necked

4. Large river

5. An important field crop

6. An important field crop

7. A large city

8. The granite faces of U.S. presidents carved on Mt. Rushmore are _____ feet high.
9. Great Plains bird

10. Wild animal: _____ _____ _____

11. Most important river

12. Black Hills animals

13. South Dakota is called "The _____ State"

14. Black Hills tree

15. Wild flower

1. __ a __ __ __ __

2. __ a __ __ __ __ __ __ __ __

3. __ __ __ a __ __ __ __

4. __ __ e __ __ __ __ __

5. __ __ __ __ __ e __ __

6. __ __ e

7. __ __ __ i __     __ __ __ __

8. __ i __ __ __

9. __ __ __ i __ __ __     __ __ __ __ __ __

10. __ o __ __     __ __ __ __ __ __ __ __
    __ __ __ __

11. __ __ __ __ o __ __ __

12. __ __ __ __ o __     __ __ __ __ __

13. __ u __ __ __ __ __

14. __ u __ __ __ __ __

15. __ __ u __ __ __ __ __

*Mt. Rushmore*

## SOUTH DAKOTA ALPHABET SEARCH

### DIRECTIONS
Find at least four names of South Dakota crops, rivers, trees, wild flowers, and cities and towns that have letters of the alphabet used only once in each *individual* word.
Example: Big Sioux  (yes, because the letters are used only once in each individual word).

Crops

_____    _____

_____    _____

_____    Trees

_____

Rivers

_____    _____

Flowers

_____

_____

_____

_____

Cities, Towns

_____

_____

_____

_____

*rye*

# TENNESSEE

31. French _____ River

**DOWN**
1. Famous country music center: Grand Ole _____
3. Raleigh: probable birthplace of 17th U.S. President, Andrew _____
4. A northern border state (abbr.)
6. An eastern border state (abbr.)
7. Pioneer hero: Davy _____
11. Tallest mountain peak: _____ Dome
12. Near Pineville: birthplace of 11th U.S. President, James _____
13. Waxhaw settlement: probable birthplace of 7th U.S. President, Andrew _____
14. Important farm animals: _____ cattle
15. Called "The ____ State"
17. National Park: Great _____ Mts.
18. _____ Fork River
19. State flower
20. _____ cover about half of Tennessee.
21. U.S. leader in mining _____
22. A field crop
23. Largest city
24. State abbr.
25. Hero of Battle of King's Mt.: John _____
27. A southern border state (abbr.)
28. A southern border state (abbr.)
29. Western border state (abbr.)

## TENNESSEE CROSSWORD PUZZLE

**ACROSS**
1. Important tree
2. A northern border state (abbr.)
5. Important tree: short-leaf _____
8. Oak Ridge: world's first _____ reactor
9. World War I military hero: Sgt. Alvin C. _____
10. Ancient Indians: _____ Builders
16. Capital city
24. Dams built for electricity and flood control (1933): _____ Valley Authority
26. A southern border state (abbr.)
28. A southern border state (abbr.)
30. Daniel _____ blazed a trail called The Wilderness Road.

84

# ᴛ E N N E S S E E

NAME _____  DATE _____

## TENNESSEE RIVER PAIRS

### DIRECTIONS

All of the Tennessee river names in the rectangle are in pairs, except one. Write the name of each river pair on a blank. (Cross them off in the rectangle as you find them.) Then find the name of the river that has no pair and write it in the box.

DUCK CLINCH CUMBERLAND CANEY FORK
STONES WOLF TENNESSEE BUFFALO
BIG SANDY HATCHIE
MISSISSIPPI CUMBERLAND LOOSAHATCHIE FRENCH BROAD OBION STONES HOLSTON WOLF CLINCH
HOLSTON POWELL HIWASSEE DUCK ELK
HARPETH ELK HATCHIE SEQUATCHIE HARPETH TENNESSEE BIG SANDY POWELL
BUFFALO LOOSAHATCHIE MISSISSIPPI OBION HIWASSEE
CANEY FORK SEQUATCHIE

_____  _____

_____  _____

_____  _____

_____  _____

_____  _____

_____  _____  [ box ]

## TENNESSEE SKYSCRAPER

### DIRECTIONS

Write your answers in the boxes. The circled letters will help you.

1. Important field crop
2. Important field crop
3. Hardwood tree
4. Severe epidemic of ____ fever (1878)
5. Valuable fruit crop
6. Indian tribe
7. Large city
8. A river
9. Large city
10. Valuable fruit crop

**Grand Ole Opry**

[Grid numbered 1-10 with circled letters Y (row 1), A (row 3), I (row 7)]

## TENNESSEE WORDS IN WORDS

How many words can you make from the letters in "Big Bend State," a name sometimes given to Tennessee because the Tennessee River bends and goes through the state twice?

### BIG BEND STATE

1. _____   4. _____   7. _____   10. _____

2. _____   5. _____   8. _____

3. _____   6. _____   9. _____

**85**

NAME _____  DATE _____

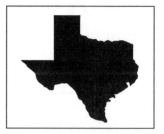

31. _____ Houston led Texans to independence from Mexico.
33. U.S. leader in growing _____ (crop)
34. The Spanish word for Texas is _____.
35. A nut crop

**DOWN**

1. An eastern border state (abbr.)
3. Jim _____ fought for independence at the Alamo.
7. Leading U.S. _____ producer (animals)
8. Called "The _____ Star State"
9. Largest city
12. Texas _____: important cattle of the 1700s and 1800s
17. Northern border state (abbr.)
18. Texas has one _____ on its flag.
19. A field crop: sugar _____
20. State abbr.
21. Davy ___ fought for independence at the Alamo.
22. Lyndon B. Johnson Space Center: headquarters for _____ (abbr.)
23. A U.S. leader in growing _____ (nuts)
24. Famous cattle trail: _____ Trail
26. Body of water on southeast boundary: _____ of Mexico
27. Southern border country
28. The _____: an old Spanish mission where a famous battle was fought
29. Large city: ___ Antonio
32. Poultry product

## TEXAS CROSSWORD PUZZLE

**ACROSS**

2. _____ ride and drive herds of cattle.
4. Western border state (abbr.)
5. An eastern border state (abbr.)
6. Texas is the _____ largest state.
7. Raised on fish farms: _____ fish
10. Capital city
11. Leading U.S. _____ producer (animal product)
13. Many Texans wear cowboy _____.
14. U.S. leader in _____ cattle
15. Important field crop
16. Large city
25. Texas _____ Hall is in Waco.
30. A tree

From *States of Wonder* published by GoodYearBooks. Copyright © 1992 Jeanne Cheyney and Arnold Cheyney.

# TEXAS

NAME _____     DATE _____

## TEXAS WORD SEARCHING

### DIRECTIONS
Find these hidden Texas words in the grid (the words not in parentheses). They can go up, down, across, at an angle, forward, or backward.

Important fruit crops:
  grapefruit
  oranges
Rivers:
  (Rio) Grande
  Red
  Brazos
  Pecos
Cities:
  (San) Antonio
  (Fort) Worth
  (Corpus) Christi
  (El) Paso
Mountains:
  Chisos
  Davis
  Guadalupe
Valuable ranch animals:
  sheep
Valuable farm crops:
  rice
  (grain) sorghum
Valuable minerals:
  helium
  petroleum
  (natural) gas
World War II hero:
  (Audie) Murphy
Early Indian tribe:
  Apache
  Comanche
Valuable trees:
  gum
  oak
  pine

| A | B | G | U | A | D | A | L | U | P | E | H | D |
|---|---|---|---|---|---|---|---|---|---|---|---|---|
| G | M | S | M | C | I | L | E | G | O | D | K | F |
| N | S | U | O | R | M | T | O | A | K | E | Q | J |
| T | G | Y | R | U | A | I | T | S | I | R | H | C |
| D | B | W | O | P | E | C | O | S | X | A | P | O |
| Z | G | K | S | I | H | C | P | V | E | T | S | M |
| S | N | F | A | N | I | Y | R | H | J | I | U | A |
| I | M | V | P | E | T | R | O | L | E | U | M | N |
| V | Y | L | A | B | W | Z | R | O | Q | R | T | C |
| A | N | T | O | N | I | O | A | X | G | F | D | H |
| D | E | R | C | J | M | E | N | Q | H | E | I | E |
| M | B | U | I | A | H | W | G | K | F | P | O | P |
| U | B | R | J | C | S | H | E | E | P | A | U | N |
| I | X | I | A | H | E | S | S | W | O | R | T | H |
| L | G | P | C | Z | E | D | N | A | R | G | K | C |
| E | A | Z | T | S | O | R | G | H | U | M | P | H |
| H | M | F | C | H | I | S | O | S | N | D | E | L |

*Alamo*

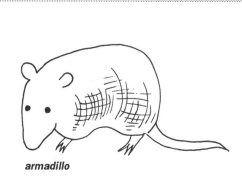

*armadillo*

87

NAME _____     DATE _____

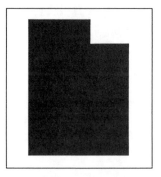

23. Great Salt Lake: water _____ and leaves salt
25. Capital and largest city: _____ Lake City
28. _____ Lake: irrigation water stored
30. The Great Salt Lake is saltier than the _____.
32. Great Salt _____ has no outlet.
33. Southern border state (abbr.)

**DOWN**
1. Some of the _____ were cut by glaciers.
2. Highest point: _____ Peak
3. _____ pioneers settled Utah in 1847.
10. Called "The _____ State"
14. Four _____ meet at the southeast corner.
16. A rocky mountain range
17. State postal abbr.
19. Present-day Indian tribe
20. UT has one of the world's largest _____ mines.
21. A famous canyon
22. Lake and stream fish
24. A tree
26. A rocky mountain range
27. Rich mineral deposits
28. An early Indian tribe
29. Eastern border state (abbr.)
31. Western border state (abbr.)

## UTAH CROSSWORD PUZZLE

**ACROSS**
1. A famous canyon: _____ Breaks
4. Rivers provide _____ for farms.
5. Most of the people live in the _____ part of Utah.
6. Irrigation water is stored in _____ Lake.
7. Famous frontiersman, trapper, and scout: Jim _____
8. A northern border state (abbr.)
9. A famous canyon
11. A northern border state (abbr.)
12. Important farm animals
13. Poultry product
15. _____ cover about a third of Utah.
18. The leading field crop

From *States of Wonder* published by GoodYearBooks. Copyright © 1992 Jeanne Cheyney and Arnold Cheyney.

# UTAH

NAME _____    DATE _____

## UTAH NAME THE TREE

### DIRECTIONS
Fill in the dotted lines with answers. If they are correct, the circled letters will spell a tree's name.

| | | |
|---|---|---|
| 1. A river | 1. | ○ _ _ _ |
| 2. Valuable liquid mineral | 2. | _ _ _ _ _ ○ _ _ |
| 3. Important poultry | 3. | _ ○ _ _ _ _ |
| 4. A large river | 4. | _ _ _ ○ _ _ |
| 5. Important mineral | 5. | ○ _ _ _ |
| 6. A national park | 6. | ○ _ _ _ _ _ _ _ _ _ _ |
| 7. A national monument | 7. _ _ _ _ _ _ _ ○ _ _ |
| 8. Large wild animal | 8. | ○ _ _ _ |
| 9. High mountains | 9. | _ _ ○ _ _ |
| 10. Important vegetable crop | 10. | _ _ _ _ _ _ ○ _ |

*deer*

## UTAH SAME FIRST LETTER

### DIRECTIONS
The circled letter is the first letter for each answer. Example:

        i   e
    ( P )  DESSERT
        u   p   p   y
        YOUNG DOG

( C )   DESERT PLANT  _ _ _ _ _
        IMPORTANT MINERAL  _ _ _ _

( B )   A NATIONAL PARK  _ _ _ _ _
        IMPORTANT CROP  _ _ _ _ _ _

( P )   IMPORTANT VEGETABLE  _ _ _ _ _ _
        IMPORTANT MINERAL  _ _ _ _ _ _ _ _ _

( A )   IMPORTANT FRUIT  _ _ _ _ _ _
        A NATIONAL PARK  _ _ _ _ _

( C )   MOST VALUABLE LIVESTOCK  _ _ _ _ _
        LARGE RIVER  _ _ _ _ _ _

( P )   FRUIT  _ _ _ _
        FRUIT  _ _ _

*seagull statue*

( G )   DESERT PLANT FOR BURNING  _ _ _ _ _ _ _
        VALUABLE MINERAL  _ _ _ _

( C )   A NATIONAL PARK  _ _ _ _ _ _ _ _ _ _
        FRUIT  _ _ _ _ _

89

# VERMONT

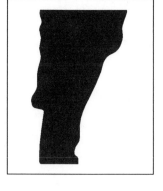

26. Field crop
27. Early Indians
28. Western border state (abbr.)
29. Birth state of 30th U.S. President, Calvin _____

**DOWN**
2. Capital city
3. Birth state of 21st U.S. President, Chester A. _____
5. Most Vermont people live in _____ areas.
7. The Champlain _____ connects Lake Champlain with the Hudson River (1823).
11. Northern border country
12. _____ cover about three-fourths of Vermont.
13. Largest city
14. Most valuable quarry mineral
15. Called "The _____ Mountain State"
16. Early American village: _____ Museum
18. Southern border state (abbr.)
22. Eastern border state (abbr.)
24. Important industry: _____ products (forests)

## VERMONT CROSSWORD PUZZLE

**ACROSS**
1. Western boundary lake
4. Leading vegetable crop
6. Eastern boundary river
8. Longest river in Vermont: _____ Creek
9. Famous Revolutionary War hero: Ethan _____
10. Concord _____: first school to train teachers
17. First permanent European settlement: Fort _____
19. A tree
20. Vermont's quiet towns

are noted for the _____ church buildings.
21. _____: Battle Monument honors colonists who defeated the British in 1777
23. State flower: _____ clover
25. State abbr.

From *States of Wonder* published by GoodYearBooks. Copyright © 1992 Jeanne Cheyney and Arnold Cheyney.

# VERMONT

NAME _____  DATE _____

## VERMONT SUPPLY THE VOWEL

### DIRECTIONS

Look for the following words in the grid (the words not in parentheses). The words can go up, down, across, at angles, backward, or forward. Parts of words may overlap. Supply the correct vowel—*a, e, i, o, u*—for the center of each word group.

(state bird: hermit) thrush
apples (most valuable fruit)
oats
milk (most valuable dairy product)
turkeys
maple (U.S. leader, syrup and sugar)
hay
corn
marble (valuable quarry product)
eggs
chickens
Lamoille (river)
Winooski (river)
(red) clover (state flower)
skiing (winter sport)
pine
Missisquoi (river)
Algonquian (early Indians)

| A | E | K | S | C | E | D | A | R | Q | O | D | K |
|---|---|---|---|---|---|---|---|---|---|---|---|---|
| H | M | T | S | F | C | N | B | X | P | M | L | M |
| H | O | Y | U | Y | T | C | S | K | I | O | N | G |
| O | R | P | B | E | V | G | U | I | M | S | N | N |
| A | B | K | P | J | B | I | R | C | N | S | A | E |
| C | L | Z | T | L | C | Y | H | W | T | I | U | B |
| H | E | C | K | A | E | T | H | R | O | S | H | A |
| I | M | P | T | N | D | S | O | Q | R | Q | T | T |
| C | Q | T | V | G | J | V | N | A | K | U | W | I |
| K | L | W | Z | L | X | O | T | I | E | O | Y | E |
| O | G | G | S | A | G | F | U | K | Y | I | L | N |
| N | L | B | G | L | K | C | I | S | S | L | O | N |
| S | W | P | A | T | V | R | L | O | I | Z | X | T |
| T | D | S | A | C | J | E | C | O | R | N | H | O |
| Y | S | T | K | M | B | G | M | N | V | A | M | L |
| D | A | S | M | J | U | A | R | I | W | E | C | N |
| P | L | V | A | T | L | X | I | W | F | Q | R | E |

bear

*apple*

# VIRGINIA

NAME _____

DATE _____

24. Important field crop
25. Large swamp near the seacoast: _____ Swamp
26. Important crop: _____ potato
27. A tree: sweet _____
28. Near Alexandria: Washington National _____
29. Near Lexington: Natural _____
30. State abbr.
31. A northeastern border state (abbr.)
32. A southern border state (abbr.)

**DOWN**

1. Great fertile valley between mountain ridges
2. Richmond: home of Confederate president Jefferson _____
3. Arlington National Cemetery: burial place of President, John F. _____
4. Northwestern border state (abbr.)
8. Hampton Roads area: important shipyards build ships for U.S. _____
11. First permanent English settlement (1607)
13. Leading crop
14. Birthplace of 4th U.S. president, James _____
16. Restored colonial town
17. Important field crop
18. Richmond, capitol building: full-size _____ of George Washington
19. Captain John _____: leader at Jamestown (1607)
21. Yorktown, 1781: Cornwallis surrendered to George _____
23. Capital city
25. Near Alexandria: _____ International Airport

## VIRGINIA CROSSWORD PUZZLE

**ACROSS**

1. Arlington National Cemetery: Tomb of the Unknown _____
3. Western border state (abbr.)
5. Great Coastal Bay: _____ Bay
6. Arlington: home of Civil War Confederate commander Robert E. _____
7. Mount _____: home of George Washington
9. A southern border state (abbr.)
10. Scenic ridge of mountains: Blue _____
12. Western route for pioneers: Cumberland _____
15. A river
20. Most important mined mineral
22. Southeast boundary ocean

# VIRGINIA

NAME _____     DATE _____

## VIRGINIA NAME THE PRESIDENT

**DIRECTIONS**
Fill in the dotted lines with answers. If they are correct, the letters will spell a president's name.

*Capt. John Smith*

1. A coastal area that is low, marshy, and water-saturated
2. Civil War peace treaty was signed at _____.
3. George Washington was elected _____ (1789).
4. The 1st president, born in VA
5. The 4th president, born in VA
6. The 5th president, born in VA
7. A famous national cemetery
8. Birthplace and early home of Robert E. Lee
9. The 9th president, born in VA
10. Virginia is called "Old _____."

## VIRGINIA SCRAMBLED WORDS

**DIRECTIONS**
Unscramble the words and write the answers on the lines provided. (Use scrap paper to work out your answers.)

1. Virginia's largest city is **K R O L N F O**. _____

2. Monticello was the home of President **S F J R N O F E E**. _____

3. How many U.S. presidents were born in Virginia? **I T G H E** _____

4. Virginia's most important livestock are **E F B E  E T L C T A**. _____   _____

5. Virginia is famous for its Smithfield **M A S H**. _____

6. An important Virginia field crop is **N O E S Y A S B**. _____

7. An important Virginia field crop is **E S P N T A U**. _____

8. A northeastern river is the **T O O C P M A**. _____

*flounder*

## VIRGINIA WORDS IN WORDS

How many words can you make from the letters in "Mother of Presidents," the nickname for Virginia? (Eight presidents were born there.)

**MOTHER OF PRESIDENTS**

1. _____
2. _____
3. _____
4. _____
5. _____
6. _____
7. _____
8. _____
9. _____
10. _____

**93**

# WASHINGTON

29. A river
30. Western boundary ocean

**DOWN**
2. A leading U.S. forest crop
3. The largest U.S. concrete dam: Grand _____
4. Seattle tower that is 607 feet high: Space _____
7. A wild animal: bob_____
8. Explorers Lewis and _____ crossed the Rockies to the Pacific (1805).
10. Leading U.S. state for growing _____ (fruit)
11. A waterfall
12. A volcano that erupted in 1980: Mt. St. _____
13. A large game animal
14. Favorite winter mountain sport
15. State bird: willow _____ finch
16. Loggers float logs to _____ mills.
17. Northern boundary country
19. Capital city
20. Important greenhouse product: flower _____
24. A leading _____ building state
26. Southern border state (abbr.)
27. Washington and the U.S. government use forest _____ conservation.

## WASHINGTON CROSSWORD PUZZLE

**ACROSS**
1. Important livestock: beef _____
3. A field crop
5. Eastern border state (abbr.)
6. A coastal fish
7. One of the longest U.S. rivers
9. Largest city
13. Many _____ on the Columbia River provide water, irrigation, and power.
18. Washington: chief U.S. provider of _____ (fish)
21. Bellingham, Seattle, and Tacoma are ports on _____ Sound.
22. State abbr.
23. A river
25. Seattle: the _____ Company manufactures airplanes
28. Highest mountain peak

*salmon*

From *States of Wonder* published by GoodYearBooks. Copyright © 1992 Jeanne Cheyney and Arnold Cheyney.

# WASHINGTON

NAME _____  DATE _____

## WASHINGTON CROSSING OVER

**DIRECTIONS**

Use a pencil for this game. Find words from the following list that have the correct number of spaces and letters to fit into the crossing-over boxes (the words not in parentheses). Each word has a place where it belongs. The first word is done for you. To continue, find a 7-letter word with "n" in the fourth space, and so on. All the words tell about Washington.

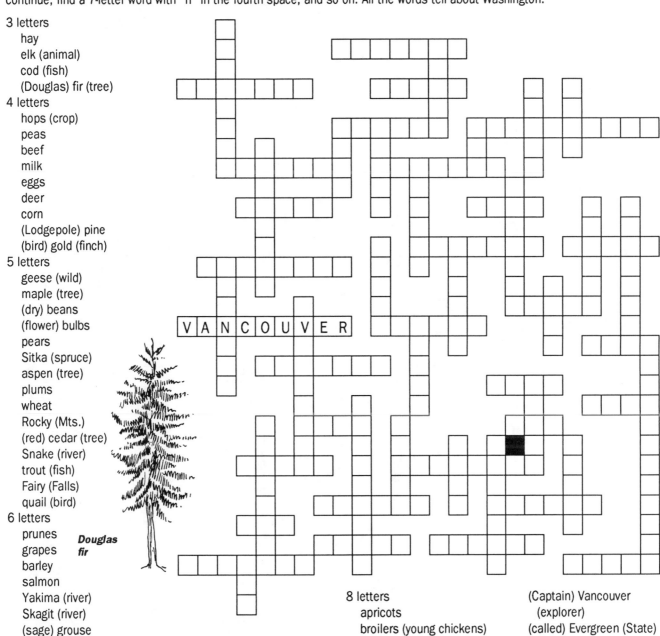

Douglas fir

**3 letters**
 hay
 elk (animal)
 cod (fish)
 (Douglas) fir (tree)

**4 letters**
 hops (crop)
 peas
 beef
 milk
 eggs
 deer
 corn
 (Lodgepole) pine
 (bird) gold (finch)

**5 letters**
 geese (wild)
 maple (tree)
 (dry) beans
 (flower) bulbs
 pears
 Sitka (spruce)
 aspen (tree)
 plums
 wheat
 Rocky (Mts.)
 (red) cedar (tree)
 Snake (river)
 trout (fish)
 Fairy (Falls)
 quail (bird)

**6 letters**
 prunes
 grapes
 barley
 salmon
 Yakima (river)
 Skagit (river)
 (sage) grouse

**7 letters**
 berries
 logging (forest industry)
 halibut (fish)
 Olympic (Mts.: rain forest)
 forests (cover over half of WA)

 alfalfa (feed)
 Cascade (Waterfalls and Mts.)
 Spokane (city)
 Tacoma (city)
 Rainbow (Falls)
 hemlock (tree)

**8 letters**
 apricots
 broilers (young chickens)
 Columbia (river)
 Colville (river)
 cherries
 sawmills

**9 letters**
 asparagus

 (Captain) Vancouver (explorer)
 (called) Evergreen (State)

**10 letters**
 cottonwood (tree)

**12 letters**
 rhododendron

VANCOUVER

NAME _____    DATE _____

27. National Historical
    Park: _____ Ferry
29. _____ cover four-fifths
    of West Virginia.
30. Southeastern border
    state (abbr.)

**DOWN**
2. Northwestern boundary
   river
3. Capital and largest city
4. Southwestern border
   state (abbr.)
7. A city producing iron
   and steel
8. State abbr.
9. The _____ Mts. cut
   through eastern West
   Virginia.
10. Ripley: state Arts and
    _____ Fair
11. _____ transport coal on
    the Ohio River.
12. River and stream fish:
    walleyed _____
13. Earliest Indians: _____
    Builders
14. Large wild animal:
    _____ bear
16. Valuable livestock:
    _____ cattle
17. Most West Virginia
    people live in _____
    areas.
18. Early Indians
19. Called "The ___ State"
20. River and stream fish
21. Important field crop
23. A northern border state
    (abbr.)
28. A northern border state
    (abbr.)

## WEST VIRGINIA CROSSWORD PUZZLE

**ACROSS**
1. A U.S. leader in soft
   _____ mining
3. Early Indians
5. Northwestern border
   state (abbr.)
6. Early Indians
13. Parkersburg: glass
    _____ center of the U.S.
15. Pottery and glassware
    are manufactured in
    _____ (a northern West
    Virginia city).
22. Coal workers united to
    form the _____ Mine

Workers of America for
better working
conditions (1890).
24. State tree: _____ maple
25. Pottery and glassware
    are manufactured in
    _____ (a western West
    Virginia city).
26. Important fruit crop

# WEST VIRGINIA

## WEST VIRGINIA RIVER AND CREEK PAIRS

**DIRECTIONS**
All of the West Virginia river and creek names in the rectangle are in pairs, except one. Write the name of each river or creek pair on a blank. (Cross them off in the rectangle as you find them.) Then find the name of the river that has no pair and write it in the box.

```
MILL   OHIO   CHEAT   GREENBRIER   BLUESTONE   WEST FORK
                                                           GUYANDOTTE
NEW    LOST   BIG SANDY      NEW      GAULEY
              MUD                                 POTOMAC
       TYGART VALLEY                    MILL
POCATALICO        WEST FORK   MEADOW  SHENANDOAH  OPEQUON  BIRCH
PATTERSON  GAULEY  ELK  TUG FORK  POTOMAC  BIRCH
KANAWHA                OPEQUON  PATTERSON   LOST    GUYANDOTTE  ELK
       MEADOW  CHEAT  POCATALICO  TYGART VALLEY  BIG SANDY  TUG FORK
MUD  BLUESTONE   GREENBRIER      KANAWHA   OHIO
```

_____     _____

_____     _____

_____     _____

_____     _____

_____     _____

_____     _____

_____     _____

_____     _____

_____     [                    ]

*marbles*

## WEST VIRGINIA ALPHABET SEARCH

**DIRECTIONS**
Find at least four names of West Virginia farm products, rivers, cities and towns, and animals that have letters of the alphabet used only once in each *individual* word. Example: Big Sandy (yes, because the letters are used only once in each individual word).

| Farm Products | Rivers | Cities, Towns |
|---|---|---|
| _____ | _____ | _____ |
| _____ | _____ | _____ |
| _____ | _____ | _____ |
| _____ | _____ | _____ |

## WEST VIRGINIA WORDS IN WORDS

How many words can you make from the letters in "Monongahela," the name of the national forest within West Virginia?

*coal miner*

**MONONGAHELA**

1. _____   5. _____   9. _____   13. _____

2. _____   6. _____   10. _____   14 _____

3. _____   7. _____   11. _____

4. _____   8. _____   12. _____

# WISCONSIN

NAME _____   DATE _____

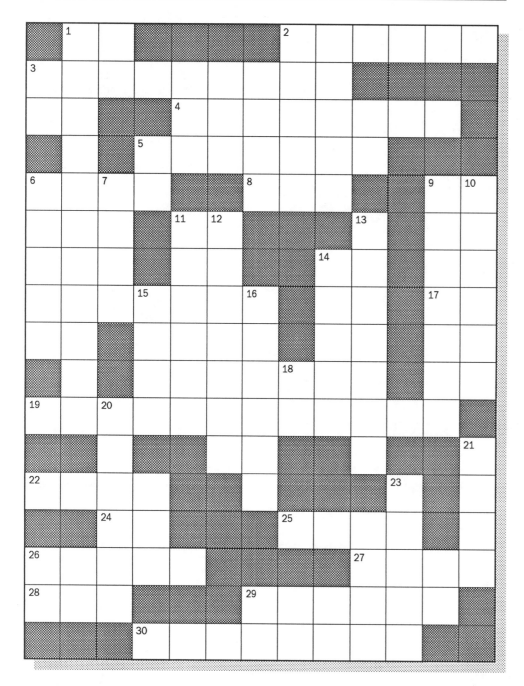

25. Popular vacation place: _____ County
26. Leading U.S. state in growing snap _____
27. Leading U.S. state in canning this vegetable
28. Important farm crop
29. William Horlick invented _____ milk in Racine in 1887.
30. Eastern boundary Great Lake: Lake _____

**DOWN**

1. Western boundary river
2. Leading U.S. state in growing this vegetable
3. A western border state (abbr.)
6. Horicon _____: large resting area for migrating Canada geese
7. Important crop: _____ beans
9. Capital city
10. State flower: Wood _____
11. Valuable dairy product
12. A pro-football team: Green Bay _____
13. _____ cover almost half of Wisconsin.
14. An important manufactured forest product
15. Small wild animal: _____chuck
16. Called "The ___ State"
18. A western boundary state (abbr.)
20. Visitor attraction: Little _____ (Norwegian homestead of the early 1800s)
21. Valuable livestock
23. The deepest lake

## WISCONSIN CROSSWORD PUZZLE

**ACROSS**

1. Northern border state (abbr.)
2. Valuable dairy product
3. Largest city
4. Northern boundary Great Lake: Lake _____
5. Highest waterfall: Big _____ Falls
6. Leading U.S. state in _____ production (dairy product)
8. A tree
17. Southern border state (abbr.)
19. The nation's first _____ for young children
22. Leading U.S. state in canning this vegetable: sweet _____
24. State abbr.

98

NAME _____ DATE _____

## WISCONSIN NUMBER CODE

### DIRECTIONS
Look at the numbers under each line. Then find the matching number in the code box and write the letters on the answer lines.

| | |
|---|---|
| A – 1 | |
| B – 2 | |
| C – 3 | |
| D – 4 | |
| E – 5 | |
| F – 6 | |
| G – 7 | |
| H – 8 | |
| I – 9 | |
| J – 10 | |
| K – 11 | |
| L – 12 | |
| M – 13 | |
| N – 14 | |
| O – 15 | |
| P – 16 | |
| Q – 17 | |
| R – 18 | |
| S – 19 | |
| T – 20 | |
| U – 21 | |
| V – 22 | |
| W – 23 | |
| X – 24 | |
| Y – 25 | |
| Z – 26 | |

**1. What is Wisconsin's title?**

1 13 5 18 9 3 1 19 ,    4 1 9 18 25 12 1 14 4

*cheese*

**2. What has fourteen rooms?**

3 1 22 5    15 6    20 8 5    13 15 21 14 4 19 ,    23 9 20 8

3 15 12 15 18 6 21 12    19 20 15 14 5    6 15 18 13 1 20 9 15 14 19

**3. Where can you go deep-sea fishing and what can you catch?**

1 16 15 19 20 12 5    9 19 12 1 14 4 19 :    3 1 20 3 8

20 18 15 21 20    1 14 4    19 1 12 13 15 14

**4. What has twenty-two rooms?**

8 15 21 19 5    15 14    20 8 5    18 15 3 11    20 8 5

18 15 3 11    9 19    450    6 5 5 20    8 9 7 8

**5. In Indian language the word *Wisconsin* has three possible meanings. What are they?**

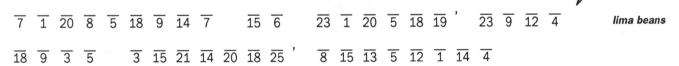

7 1 20 8 5 18 9 14 7    15 6    23 1 20 5 18 19 ,    23 9 12 4

18 9 3 5    3 15 21 14 20 18 25 ,    8 15 13 5 12 1 14 4

*lima beans*

**6. Why is Wisconsin called "The Badger State"?**

(1820)

19 15 13 5    12 5 1 4    13 9 14 5 18 19    12 9 22 5 4    9 14

3 1 22 5 19    4 21 7    15 21 20    15 6    20 8 5

8 9 12 12 19 9 4 5 19 ,    12 9 11 5    2 21 18 18 15 23 9 14 7

2 1 4 7 5 18 19 .

# WYOMING

NAME _____     DATE _____

24. First U.S. woman
    _____, Nellie Ross
    (1925)
26. A small wild animal
27. A southern border state
    (abbr.)
28. Most valuable
    livestock: _____ cattle
32. Many rivers have cut
    deep _____.
33. First U.S. national
    monument: Devil's _____

**DOWN**

3. Half of Wyoming is
   used to graze _____.
4. Important ranch
   animals
6. Early Indians
7. Largest city
9. Wild animal: wild_____
11. World's largest and
    oldest national park
12. The _____ Trail crosses
    the state.
15. Tourist attraction in
    Yellowstone National
    Park: Old Faithful _____
16. Northern border state
    (abbr.)
18. Capital city
19. Important tree: Douglas
    _____
20. Valuable ranch product:
    _____ (sheep product)
21. (July) Cheyenne, most
    popular yearly state
    event: _____ Days
23. Where pioneers carved
    their names:
    Independence _____
25. An eastern border state
    (abbr.)
29. Near Jackson: National
    _____ Refuge
30. Leading field crop
31. State abbr.

# WYOMING CROSSWORD PUZZLE

**ACROSS**

1. Western border state
   (abbr.)
2. Huge range of rugged
   mountains
5. National Historic Site:
   Fort _____
7. A southern border state
   (abbr.)
8. Rugged, lonely towers
   of rock
10. A national park: Grand
    _____
13. Large wild animal:
    _____ bear
14. A leading producer of
    _____ (liquid mineral)
17. The U.S. _____ owns
    nearly half of Wyoming.
22. An eastern border state
    (abbr.)

From *States of Wonder* published by GoodYearBooks. Copyright © 1992 Jeanne Cheyney and Arnold Cheyney.

# WYOMING

NAME _____ DATE _____

## WYOMING WORD SEARCHING

### DIRECTIONS

Find these hidden Wyoming words in the grid (the words not in parentheses). They can go up, down, across, at an angle, forward, or backward.

Crops:
  barley
  wheat
  (sugar) beets
  corn
  beans
Large mineral deposits:
  coal
  uranium
Some early Indian tribes:
  Arapaho
  Blackfeet
  Crow
  Sioux
  Ute
  Cheyenne
Rivers:
  (North) Platte
  Niobrara
  Yellowstone
  Clarks (Fork)
  Tongue
  Bighorn
  Powder
Cities:
  Laramie
  Casper
  Sheridan
  (Rock) Springs

| L | B | E | N | O | T | S | W | O | L | L | E | Y |
|---|---|---|---|---|---|---|---|---|---|---|---|---|
| D | A | M | B | I | F | Q | J | C | R | N | O | G |
| K | S | R | E | P | S | A | C | L | A | R | K | S |
| A | U | W | A | Z | P | T | O | X | E | U | H | T |
| E | R | C | N | M | R | C | A | L | G | P | D | E |
| L | A | H | S | K | I | H | L | J | O | I | Y | E |
| F | N | A | N | V | N | E | P | B | H | O | M | B |
| T | I | Q | Y | S | G | Y | A | R | A | W | V | S |
| B | U | E | D | I | S | E | G | J | P | F | H | B |
| L | M | H | E | U | G | N | O | T | A | E | M | K |
| A | L | N | C | T | N | N | R | C | R | O | W | R |
| C | S | R | V | E | T | E | E | I | A | Y | O | E |
| K | C | O | R | N | O | G | D | H | P | U | B | T |
| F | C | H | A | I | N | A | W | W | H | E | A | T |
| E | J | G | E | K | N | I | O | B | R | A | R | A |
| E | S | I | O | U | X | R | P | T | L | F | O | L |
| T | D | B | A | R | L | E | Y | M | A | P | S | P |

*eagle*

*Old Faithful*

# TOURISM ADDRESSES

Alabama Bureau of Tourism
and Travel
532 South Perry Street
Montgomery, AL 36103

Alaska Tourism Marketing
Council
P. O. Box E-501
Juneau, AK 99811

Arizona Office of Tourism
1100 West Washington
Phoenix, AZ 85007

Arkansas Department of
Parks & Tourism
One Capitol Mall
Little Rock, AR 72201

California Office of Tourism
1121 L St., Suite 103
Sacramento, CA 95814

Colorado Tourism Board
P. O. Box 38700
Denver, CO 80238

Connecticut Department of
Economic Development
210 Washington St.
Hartford, CT 06106

Delaware Tourism Office
99 Kings Highway
P. O. Box 1401
Dover, DE 19903

Florida Department of
Commerce
Florida Visitor Inquiry
126 Van Buren Street
Tallahassee, FL 32399-2000

Georgia Tourist Division
230 Peachtree Street, NW
Atlanta, GA 30303

Hawaii Visitors Bureau
441 Lexington Avenue
New York, NY 10017

Idaho Travel Council
Administrative Office
Idaho Department of Com-
merce
700 West State Street
Boise, ID 83720

Illinois Office of Tourism
Department of Commerce and
Community Affairs
310 South Michigan Avenue
Chicago, IL 60604

Indiana Department of
Commerce
Tourism Development Division
One N. Capitol, Suite 700
Indianapolis, IN 46204-2288

Iowa Department of Economic
Development
200 East Grand Avenue
Des Moines, IA 50309

Kansas Department of
Commerce
400 W. 8th, 5th Floor
Topeka, KS 66603-3957

Kentucky Department of
Travel Development
Capital Plaza Tower
Frankfort, KY 40601

Louisiana Office of Tourism
Department of Culture,
Recreation, and Tourism
P. O. Box 94291
Baton Rouge, LA 70804-9291

Maine Tourism Information
Services
The Maine Publicity Bureau,
Inc.
97 Winthrop Street
P. O. Box 2300
Hallowell, ME 04347-2300

Maryland Department of
Economic & Employment
Development
Office of Tourism Develop-
ment
217 East Redwood Street
Baltimore, MD 21202

Massachusetts Division of
Tourism
Department of Commerce
100 Cambridge Street, 13th
Floor
Boston, MA 02202

Michigan Travel Bureau
Department of Commerce
P. O. Box 30226
Lansing, MI 48909

Minnesota Office of Tourism
375 Jackson St., 250 Skyway
Level
St. Paul, MN 55101-1810

Mississippi Department of
Economic and Community
Development
Division of Tourism
P. O. Box 849
Jackson, MS 39205-0849

Missouri Division of Tourism
Truman State Office Building
P. O. Box 1055
Jefferson City, MO 65102

Montana Travel
Department of Commerce
Helena, MT 59620

Nebraska Department of
Economic Development
Division of Travel & Tourism
301 Centennial Mall South,
Box 94666
Lincoln, NE 68509

Nevada Commission of
Tourism
Capitol Complex
Carson City, NV 89710

State of New Hampshire
Office of Vacation Travel
P. O. Box 856
Concord, NH 03301

New Jersey Division of Travel
and Tourism
20 W. State Street, CN 826
Trenton, NJ 08625

New Mexico Economic
Development & Tourism
Department
Joseph Montoya Bldg.
P. O. Box 20003
1100 St. Francis Dr.
Santa Fe, NM 87503

New York State Department
of Economic Development
One Commerce Plaza
Albany, NY 12245

North Carolina Division of
Travel and Tourism
Department of Commerce
430 North Salisbury Street
Raleigh, NC 27611

North Dakota Tourism
Promotion
State Capitol Grounds
Bismarck, ND 58505

Ohio Department of Develop-
ment
P. O. Box 1001
Columbus, OH 43266-0101

Oklahoma Tourism and
Recreation Department
500 Will Rogers Building
Oklahoma City, OK 73105

Oregon Economic Develop-
ment Department
595 Cottage Street N.E.
Salem, OR 97310

Pennsylvania Department of
Commerce
P. O. Box 61
Warrendale, PA 15086

Rhode Island Department of
Economic Development
7 Jackson Walkway
Providence, RI 02903

South Carolina Division of
Tourism
P. O. Box 71
Columbia, SC 29202-0071

South Dakota Tourism
Capitol Lake Plaza
Pierre, SD 57501

Tennessee Tourist Develop-
ment
P. O. Box 23170
Nashville, TN 37202

Texas Department of
Highways and Public
Transportation
P. O. Box 5064
Austin, TX 78763-5064

Utah Travel Council
Council Hall/Capitol Hill
Salt Lake City, UT 84114

Vermont Travel Division
Montpelier, VT 05602

Virginia Division of Tourism
202 N. Ninth St., Suite 500
Richmond, VA 23219

Washington State Department
of Trade and Economic
Development
Tourism Development
Division
101 General Administration
Bldg. AX-13
Olympia, WA 98504-0613

West Virginia Department of
Tourism
Capitol Building
Charleston, WV 25305

Wisconsin Division of Tourism
P. O. Box 7606
Madison, WI 53707

Wyoming Travel Commission
I-25 at College Drive
Cheyenne, WY 82002

From States of Wonder published by GoodYearBooks. Copyright © 1992 Jeanne Cheyney and Arnold Cheyney.

# CROSSWORD AND GAME GRID

# ANSWERS

## ALABAMA CROSSWORD PUZZLE

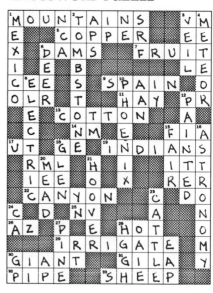

## ALASKA CROSSWORD PUZZLE

## ARIZONA CROSSWORD PUZZLE

## ALABAMA WORD SEARCHING

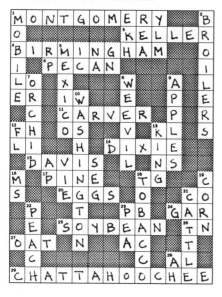

## ALASKA PAIRS OF ISLAND NAMES

| | |
|---|---|
| Adak | Montague |
| Agattu | Nunivak |
| Amchitka | Rat |
| Amlia | St. George |
| Andreanof | St. Lawrence |
| Attu | St. Matthew |
| Chirikof | St. Paul |
| Four Mountains | Sanak |
| Fox | Tanaga |
| Kiska | Trinity |
| Middleton | Unimak |

| Kodiak |
|---|

## ALASKA NAME THE CITY

1. **F**orest
2. e**A**gles
3. ferry**ll**ner
4. Be**R**ing
5. grizzly **B**ear
6. Aleuti**A**n
7. chicke**N**s
8. mil**K**
9. **S**eward

## ARIZONA CROSSING OVER

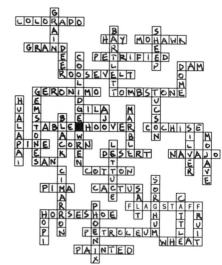

## ARKANSAS CROSSWORD PUZZLE

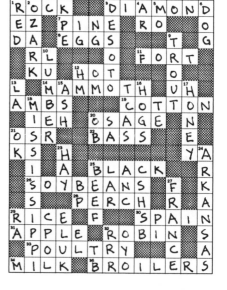

## ARKANSAS NUMBER CODE

1. Crater of Diamonds State Park: an active diamond mine near Murfreesboro. Tourists who find diamonds there may keep them.
2. the largest government trout hatchery in the U.S.
3. Caddo   Osage   Quapaw
4. Hernando de Soto, a Spanish explorer, crossed the Mississippi R. and went across Arkansas to the Ozarks.
5. Arkansas River

## CALIFORNIA
## CROSSWORD PUZZLE

## CALIFORNIA NAME THE CITY

1.         Lo**S** Angeles
2.         **SA**n Joaquin
3. San Fran**C**isco
4.         ho**R**ses
5.         or**A**nge
6.         Yose**M**ite
7.         b**E**ef cattle
8.         Dis**N**eyland
9.         Dea**T**h Valley
10.        **GO**lden Gate

## CALIFORNIA
## SCRAMBLED MOUNTAINS

1. Red
2. Chocolate
3. Salmon
4. San Bernardino
5. San Rafael
6. Santa Cruz
7. Sierra Nevada
8. Frazier

## COLORADO
## CROSSWORD PUZZLE

## COLORADO
## SUPPLY THE VOWEL

## CONNECTICUT
## CROSSWORD PUZZLE

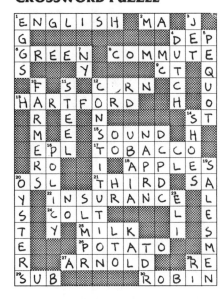

## CONNECTICUT MORSE CODE

1. the first cookbook written by an American: American Cookery.
2. Mystic Seaport: In the harbor is New England's last wooden whaling ship.
3. Lake Candlewood: It was made to store water for generating power.
4. Connecticut River

## DELAWARE
## CROSSWORD PUZZLE

## DELAWARE CROSSING OVER

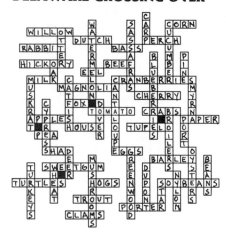

## FLORIDA
## CROSSWORD PUZZLE

## FLORIDA NAME THE CITY

1. **ST**. Augustine
2. J**A**cksonville
3. Pe**L**ican Island
4. **O**range Bow**L**
5. tom**A**to
6. St. Jo**H**ns
7. Atl**A**ntic Ocean
8. poin**S**ettia
9. Silver **S**prings
10. Ok**E**echobee
11. **E**gret

## FLORIDA SKYSCRAPER

1. L
2. FL
3. red
4. corn
5. melon
6. Panama
7. peanuts
8. Seminole
9. tangerine
10. Petersburg

## GEORGIA
## CROSSWORD PUZZLE

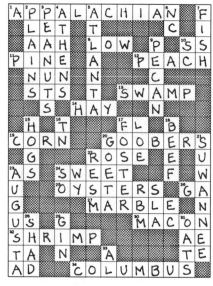

## GEORGIA WORD SEARCHING

## HAWAII
## CROSSWORD PUZZLE

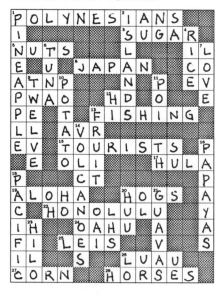

## HAWAII FOOD PAIRS

| | |
|---|---|
| avocado | nuts |
| bananas | papaya |
| beans | pineapple |
| cabbage | potatoes |
| cattle | poultry |
| coffee | rice |
| corn | sugar |
| guava | taro |
| hogs | tuna |

poi

## HAWAII SCRAMBLED WORDS

1. military bases
2. bombed
3. black
4. people
5. cattle, hogs
6. flowers
7. coffee
8. beans, bananas

From *States of Wonder* published by GoodYearBooks. Copyright © 1992 Jeanne Cheyney and Arnold Cheyney.

## IDAHO CROSSWORD PUZZLE

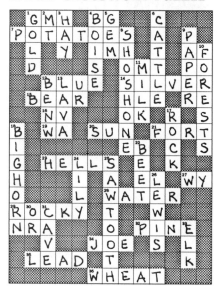

### IDAHO CLUE

Forest trees:
- cedar
- spruce
- hemlock
- aspen
- pine
- fir
- birch

Chief rivers:
- Snake
- Salmon

Wild animals:
- bear
- otter
- beaver
- moose
- raccoon
- coyote
- bobcat
- cougar

Cities:
- Coeur d'Alene
- Nampa
- Twin Falls
- Pocatello

An abandoned mining town:
- ghost town

Early Indian tribes:
- Shoshone
- Bannock

### IDAHO SAME FIRST LETTER

**B** Boise
  Blackfoot
**C** Cache
  Clearwater
**S** Snake
  Salmon

**C** Challis
  Caribou
**B** Boise
  Bruneau
**P** Payette
  Priest

## ILLINOIS CROSSWORD PUZZLE

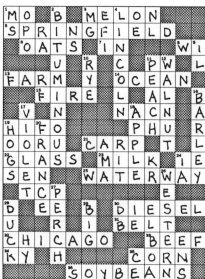

### ILLINOIS NUMBER CODE

1. the home of Ulysses S. Grant, 18th U.S. President
2. Ronald Reagan
3. Dickson Mounds: partly opened Indian mounds with Indian skeletons
4. farm machinery
5. diesel engines
6. He lived in Springfield.

## INDIANA CROSSWORD PUZZLE

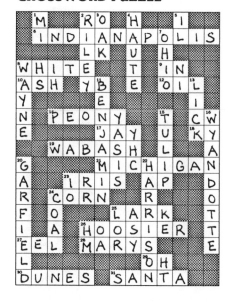

## INDIANA SUPPLY THE VOWEL

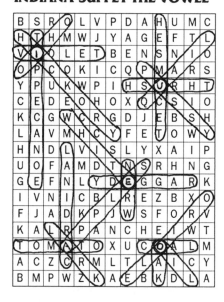

## IOWA CROSSWORD PUZZLE

### IOWA SKYSCRAPER

1. R
2. IA
3. fox
4. Hawk
5. farms
6. rabbit
7. Hawkeye
8. marigold
9. goldfinch
10. cottonwood
11. Nishnabotna

# KANSAS CROSSWORD PUZZLE

# KENTUCKY CROSSWORD PUZZLE

## LOUISIANA CLUE

Important rivers:
    Sabine
    Calcasieu
    Mississippi
Birds:
    egret
    turkey
    pelican
Wild animals:
    alligator
    beaver
    wildcat
Freshwater fish:
    bass
    catfish
    sunfish
Ocean fish:
    rays
    tarpon

## KANSAS
## NAME THE STATE BIRD

1. **W**yatt Earp
2. sunflow**E**r
3. Mis**S**ouri
4. whea**T**
5. prairi**E** dog
6. prai**R**ie chicken
7. airpla**N**es

8. flour **M**illing
9. b**E**ef cattle
10. gr**A**in sorghum
11. **D**uck
12. Ne**O**sho
13. **W**oodpecker
14. Wild Bi**L**l Hickok
15. Bat M**A**sterson
16. **R**attlesnake
17. **K**ansas City

## KENTUCKY CROSSING OVER

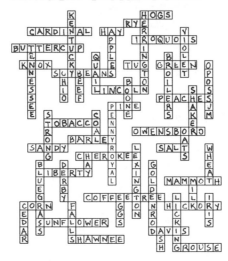

## LOUISIANA NUMBER CODE

1. an egret (bird) sanctuary
2. Jean Lafitte: Grand Isle
3. crayfish

## MAINE CROSSWORD PUZZLE

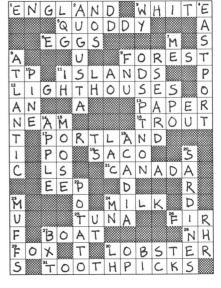

## KANSAS SCRAMBLED WORDS

Wild flowers
    thistle
    clover
    daisy
Birds
    robin
    hawk
    crow
Wild animals
    rabbit
    raccoon
    muskrat

## LOUISIANA CROSSWORD PUZZLE

From States of Wonder published by GoodYearBooks. Copyright © 1992 Jeanne Cheyney and Arnold Cheyney.

## MAINE WORD SEARCHING

| | | | | | | | | | | | | |
|---|---|---|---|---|---|---|---|---|---|---|---|---|
| R | B | A | S | B | S | G | N | I | D | D | E | W |
| D | I | X | B | T | F | Q | D | S | Y | F | B | N |
| A | R | H | N | R | O | B | J | I | G | X | I | A |
| E | C | W | M | A | P | L | E | K | Q | G | C | R |
| H | H | K | E | P | M | H | W | S | G | T | H | O |
| E | S | E | K | S | J | P | L | O | O | N | I | K |
| S | K | P | M | B | E | E | C | H | Z | M | C | A |
| O | C | K | P | L | T | S | F | J | N | I | K | E |
| O | I | P | E | N | O | B | S | C | O | T | A | G |
| M | T | K | S | R | Y | C | Z | Y | W | A | D | E |
| X | S | E | D | S | S | A | K | I | F | O | E | S |
| S | L | N | G | E | Y | Z | V | T | O | C | E | O |
| P | A | N | B | O | X | E | S | W | F | H | D | S |
| R | X | E | C | N | Z | N | S | S | C | O | A | F |
| U | P | B | O | A | K | S | E | T | J | C | I | A |
| C | E | E | J | C | A | L | A | H | D | A | O | B |
| E | M | C | Q | B | R | M | Y | D | K | S | H | V |

## MARYLAND CROSSWORD PUZZLE

| | | | | | | | | | | | | |
|---|---|---|---|---|---|---|---|---|---|---|---|---|
| C | H | E | S | A | P | E | A | K | E | | E | |
| | | L | I | N | E | | P | A | | W | L | |
| S | U | S | A | N | | | P | | O | A | K | |
| M | D | | N | A | V | A | L | | | S | | |
| | D | E | | P | | K | E | Y | | H | A | Y |
| B | | | C | O | R | N | | | M | I | L | K |
| A | P | P | A | L | A | C | H | I | A | N | | |
| L | E | | | I | | | | H | O | G | S | |
| T | R | | | S | T | O | N | E | | T | | O |
| I | C | | | | R | | | | B | O | | Y |
| M | H | T | | W | E | S | T | E | R | N | | S |
| O | | O | T | T | E | R | | | O | | | T |
| R | | B | | | S | | B | R | I | D | G | E |
| E | | A | S | H | | M | A | P | L | E | | R |
| | | C | | | | F | O | R | E | S | T | S |
| | | C | L | A | M | S | | | R | | | |
| | S | O | Y | B | E | A | N | | S | | V | A |

## MARYLAND RIVER AND CREEK PAIRS

| | |
|---|---|
| Antietam | Pocomoke |
| Chester | Potomac |
| Choptank | Sassafras |
| Conococheague | Severn |
| Elk | South |
| Gunpowder | Susquehanna |
| Monocracy | Wicomico |
| Nanticoke | Youghiogheny |
| Patuxent | |

Northeast

## MARYLAND SCRAMBLED WORDS

1. rockfish
2. Civil War battlefield
3. settlement: St. Mary's City
4. gemstones
5. umbrella
6. white oak tree
7. Confederate

## MASSACHUSETTS CROSSWORD PUZZLE

| | | | | | | | | | | | | |
|---|---|---|---|---|---|---|---|---|---|---|---|---|
| B | O | S | T | O | N | | P | L | A | N | T | S |
| A | | | S | C | A | L | L | O | P | | E | |
| Y | | E | | | | N | Y | | | E | L | M |
| | M | G | | C | L | A | M | S | | | E | Y |
| H | I | G | H | | | P | O | S | T | | P | S |
| A | L | S | | M | I | N | U | T | E | | H | T |
| R | K | | | | | C | T | | | | O | I |
| B | | B | | W | | | H | | N | | N | C |
| O | | A | D | A | M | S | | | A | | E | |
| R | | S | | R | | W | | | N | S | | |
| S | | K | | | | O | | | T | A | | K |
| | B | E | D | F | O | R | D | | U | U | | E |
| | | T | E | A | | D | E | | C | G | | N |
| | | B | | | N | | E | | K | U | | N |
| C | R | A | N | B | E | R | R | I | E | S | | E |
| O | I | L | H | | W | | | V | T | | | D |
| D | | L | | | S | | | | | H | A | Y |

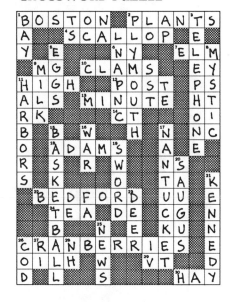

## MASSACHUSETTS NAME THE SPECIAL DAY

1. **T**aconic
2. Bunker **H**ill
3. Merrim**A**ck
4. Con**N**ecticut
5. chic**K**adee
6. **S**alem
7. **G**loucester
8. Const**I**tution
9. Paul Re**V**ere
10. Berksh**I**re Valley
11. Martha's Vi**N**eyard
12. Mt. **G**reylock

## MICHIGAN CROSSWORD PUZZLE

| | | | | | | | | | | | | |
|---|---|---|---|---|---|---|---|---|---|---|---|---|
| F | O | R | D | | D | U | C | K | S | | | B |
| O | | A | S | P | E | N | | | E | R | I | E |
| R | | | | | T | | S | A | L | T | | A |
| E | | M | I | | R | | O | A | K | | I | N |
| S | | A | U | T | O | M | O | B | I | L | E | S |
| T | | C | | | I | | | B | E | A | R | |
| S | | K | | | T | | F | L | I | N | T | |
| | P | I | N | E | | P | E | A | R | S | | |
| M | I | N | K | | | | | | M | I | L | K |
| | | A | | G | | R | O | B | I | N | | |
| | | C | E | R | E | A | L | | | G | | |
| P | | | C | A | L | V | E | S | | | | C |
| E | | A | S | P | A | R | A | G | U | S | | H |
| A | P | P | L | E | S | | | G | E | E | S | E |
| C | | | | S | O | Y | B | E | A | N | | R |
| H | O | G | S | | | | | | P | E | A | R |
| | H | O | N | E | Y | | | D | A | I | R | Y |

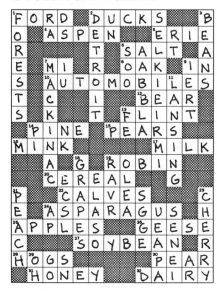

## MICHIGAN MORSE CODE

1. the first painted traffic lines on streets
2. "The Wolverine State": Fur traders brought wolverine pelts to trade.
3. robots
4. largest makers of carpet sweepers in the world
5. deer
6. Mackinac Bridge

## MINNESOTA CROSSWORD PUZZLE

| | | | | | | | | | | | | |
|---|---|---|---|---|---|---|---|---|---|---|---|---|
| | T | | P | | | H | O | G | S | | | P |
| | R | | E | | M | A | Y | O | | T | I | A |
| C | A | N | A | D | A | | | P | | W | T | U |
| N | D | | S | | | | | H | | I | A | L |
| | E | | | S | O | Y | B | E | A | N | S | |
| | R | Y | E | | | | U | R | | | C | |
| | S | D | | B | E | E | T | | | I | A | |
| D | | | | | W | A | T | E | R | | | |
| U | | | M | I | N | N | E | H | A | H | A | |
| L | | O | I | L | | | R | E | D | | | |
| U | | F | L | O | U | R | | | | C | | |
| T | T | | K | | P | O | T | A | T | O | | A |
| H | A | Y | | | | | B | E | A | R | | P |
| | P | I | N | E | | | I | R | O | N | | P |
| B | E | A | N | S | | | | | | | | L |
| | | W | I | | M | | C | H | E | E | S | E |
| | | M | I | N | N | E | A | P | O | L | I | S |

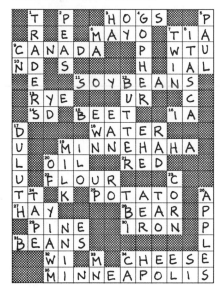

## MINNESOTA CLUE

Cities:
- Saint Cloud
- Mankato
- St. Paul
- La Crosse
- Grand Forks

Early Indian tribes:
- Sioux
- Chippewa

Big lakes:
- Minnetonka
- Winnibigoshish
- Big Stone

National forests:
- Chippewa
- Superior

Rivers:
- Crow Wing
- Otter Tail
- Big Fork

Big wild animals:
- moose
- black bear
- deer

## MINNESOTA SKYSCRAPER

1. MN
2. Red
3. cows
4. Thief
5. walnut
6. Landing
7. Snelling
8. Glensheen
9. automobile
10. thermostats

## MISSISSIPPI CROSSWORD PUZZLE

## MISSOURI CROSSWORD PUZZLE

## MISSISSIPPI SUPPLY THE VOWEL

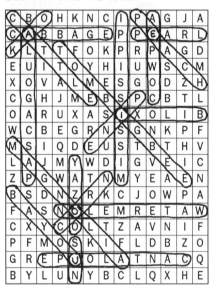

## MISSOURI CROSSING OVER

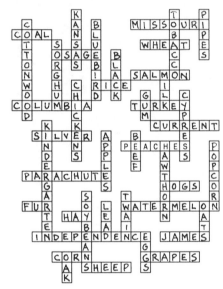

From *States of Wonder* published by GoodYearBooks. Copyright © 1992 Jeanne Cheyney and Arnold Cheyney.

## MONTANA
## CROSSWORD PUZZLE

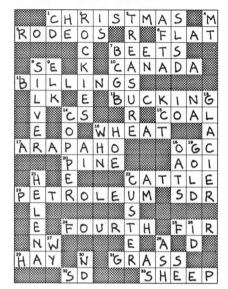

## NEBRASKA
## CROSSWORD PUZZLE

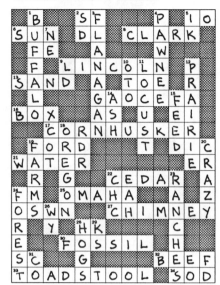

## NEVADA
## CROSSWORD PUZZLE

## MONTANA
## NAME THE OUTLAW FIGHTERS

1. beaVer
2. flr
3. Grasshopper
4. MIssouri
5. YelLowstone
6. Antelope
7. hoNey
8. bitTerroot
9. biblEs
10. mooSe

## MONTANA
## SCRAMBLED WORDS

1. black cherries
2. ponderosa pine
3. buffalo grass
4. Shoshone
5. Blackfeet
6. duck
7. bear
8. sheep

## NEBRASKA
## WORD SEARCHING

## NEVADA CLUE

Desert plants:
  cactus
  sagebrush
  yucca
Crops:
  alfalfa seed
  hay
  potatoes
  wheat
  barley
Indian tribes:
  Pueblo
  Washoe
  Mohave

Paiute
Shoshone
Wild animals:
  coyote
  fox
  marmot
  porcupine
  bighorn sheep
  badger
  muskrat
  rabbit
  snake
1. rock
2. bottles

## NEVADA
## RIVER AND CREEK PAIRS

| | |
|---|---|
| Bruneau | Pine |
| Carson | Quinn |
| Colorado | Reefe |
| East Walker | Rock |
| Humboldt | Truckee |
| Huntington | Salmon |
| Mary's | Virgin |
| Muddy | West Walker |
| Owyhee | |

White

# NEW HAMPSHIRE CROSSWORD PUZZLE

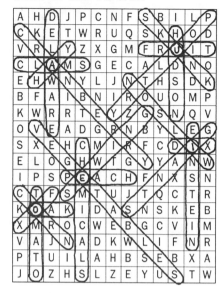

# NEW JERSEY SUPPLY THE VOWEL

# NEW MEXICO NAME THE FAMOUS NATIONAL PARK

1.  **C**hili peppers
2.  r**A**ttlesnake
3.  Ge**R**onimo
4.  mi**L**k
5.  me**S**quite
6.  **B**eef cattle
7.  yucc**A**
8.  roa**D**runner

9.  En**C**hantment
10. **A**nasazi
11. Pancho **V**illa
12. Pu**E**blo
13. **R**io Grande
14. Sa**N** Miguel
15. Peco**S**

# NEW HAMPSHIRE NUMBER CODE

1. New Hampshire minutemen raced to Boston, MA, to help fight the British.
2. skiing competitions
3. artificial rain: scientists used dry ice to "seed clouds" and cause rain over a forest fire.
4. dairy farming
5. The Algonquian Indians farmed, hunted, fished, and built wigwams of bark and skins.
   their enemy: Iroquois Indians

# NEW JERSEY CROSSWORD PUZZLE

# NEW MEXICO CROSSWORD PUZZLE

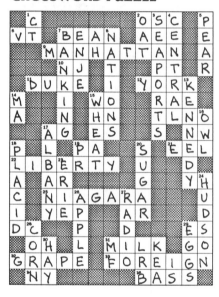

# NEW YORK CROSSWORD PUZZLE

# NEW YORK CROSSING OVER

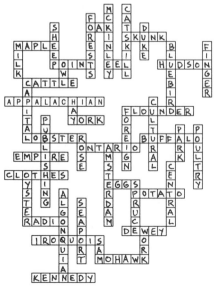

From States of Wonder published by GoodYearBooks. Copyright © 1992 Jeanne Cheyney and Arnold Cheyney.

# NORTH CAROLINA CROSSWORD PUZZLE

## NORTH CAROLINA CLUE

1. Mitchell
2. Biltmore
3. hickory
4. Tuscarora
5. furniture
6. ducks
7. Tories
8. Whigs
9. textile
10. peanuts
11. Catawba
12. Bath
13. clams
14. coastal
15. Cherokee
16. Broad
17. Piedmont
18. hogs
19. Tryon
20. soybeans
21. broilers

# NORTH DAKOTA CROSSWORD PUZZLE

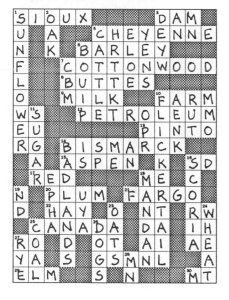

# NORTH DAKOTA WORD SEARCHING

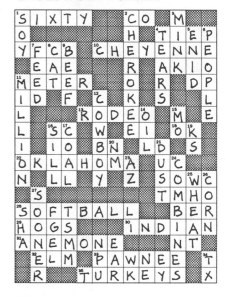

# OHIO CROSSWORD PUZZLE

## OHIO RIVER PAIRS

| | |
|---|---|
| Auglaize | Ohio |
| Blanchard | Olentangy |
| Cuyahoga | Portage |
| Grand | St. Joseph |
| Hocking | St. Mary |
| Huron | Sandusky |
| Kokosing | Scioto |
| Maumee | Tiffin |
| Miami | Vermillion |
| Mohican | Wabash |
| Muskingum | Walhonding |

Licking

# OHIO SKYSCRAPER

1. OH
2. fox
3. corn
4. match
5. tomato
6. traffic
7. McGuffey
8. Armstrong
9. Youngstown
10. Appalachian
11. Pennsylvania

# OKLAHOMA CROSSWORD PUZZLE

## OKLAHOMA SCRAMBLED WORDS

1. mesquite, sagebrush
2. Red, Arkansas
3. eggs, milk
4. peanuts, hay
5. hickory, walnut
6. buffalo herds

## OKLAHOMA SAME FIRST LETTER

**O** Ouachita
opossum

**A** armadillo
Arbuckle

**P** Poteau
prairie dog

**C** Commanche
Chisholm

**S** Stillwater
sorghum

**W** Wichita
wild indigo

**C** cotton
chicken

**C** Cimarron
Cache

**T** Tulsa
turkey

# OREGON CROSSWORD PUZZLE

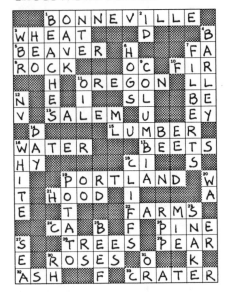

# PENNSYLVANIA CROSSWORD PUZZLE

# RHODE ISLAND CROSSWORD PUZZLE

## OREGON SUPPLY THE VOWEL

## PENNSYLVANIA NAME THE MOUNTAIN RANGE

1. **A**mish
2. **P**enn's Woods
3. **P**arade
4. **A**llegheny
5. Rockvi**L**le
6. h**A**y
7. Po**C**ono
8. mus**H**rooms
9. L**I**ncoln
10. **A**pples
11. Keysto**N**e

## PENNSYLVANIA SAME FIRST LETTER

**A** apples
　Algonquian
**Q** quiet
　Quaker
**S** Susquehanna
　Sweden
**P** peaches
　Philadelphia
**G** glassmaking
　grouse
**P** Pittsburgh
　Pine Creek

## RHODE ISLAND MORSE CODE

1. the oldest Jewish synagogue in the U.S. (still standing)
2. silverware and jewelry making
3. Rhode Island Reds, chickens: they give lots of eggs and have delicious meat
4. a mansion, Marble House, one of the most elegant U.S. buildings

## SOUTH CAROLINA CROSSWORD PUZZLE

From *States of Wonder* published by GoodYearBooks. Copyright © 1992 Jeanne Cheyney and Arnold Cheyney.

# SOUTH CAROLINA CROSSING OVER

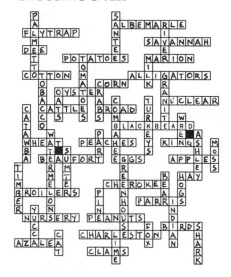

# TENNESSEE CROSSWORD PUZZLE

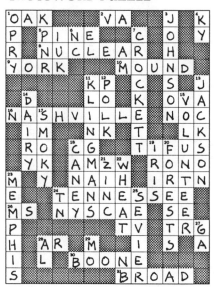

# TEXAS CROSSWORD PUZZLE

# SOUTH DAKOTA CROSSWORD PUZZLE

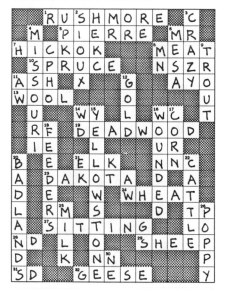

## TENNESSEE RIVER PAIRS

| | |
|---|---|
| Big Sandy | Holston |
| Buffalo | Loosahatchie |
| Caney Fork | Mississippi |
| Clinch | Obion |
| Cumberland | Powell |
| Duck | Sequatchie |
| Elk | Stones |
| Harpeth | Tennessee |
| Hatchie | Wolf |
| Hiwassee | |

French Broad

## TENNESSEE SKYSCRAPER

1. hay
2. corn
3. maple
4. yellow
5. peaches
6. Cherokee
7. Knoxville
8. Sequatchie
9. Chattanooga
10. strawberries

# TEXAS WORD SEARCHING

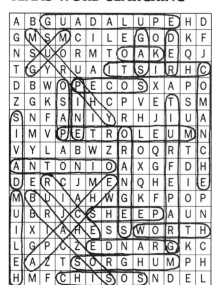

## SOUTH DAKOTA CLUE

1. Palace
2. pasqueflower
3. pheasant
4. Cheyenne
5. flaxseed
6. rye
7. Rapid City
8. sixty
9. prairie chicken
10. Rocky Mountain goat
11. Missouri
12. bighorn sheep
13. Sunshine
14. juniper
15. bluebell

# UTAH CROSSWORD PUZZLE

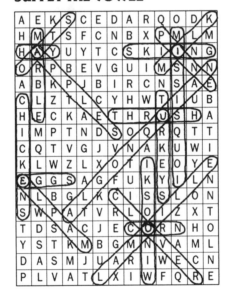

# VERMONT CROSSWORD PUZZLE

# VIRGINIA CROSSWORD PUZZLE

## UTAH NAME THE TREE

1. **B**ear
2. petro**L**eum
3. t**U**rkeys
4. Gre**E**n
5. **S**ilver
6. Ca**P**itol Reef
7. Rainbow B**R**idge
8. b**U**ffalo
9. Ro**C**ky
10. potato**E**s

## UTAH SAME FIRST LETTER

**C** cactus
   coal
**P** potato
   petroleum
**C** cattle
   Colorado
**G** greasewood
   gold
**B** Bryce
   barley
**A** apple
   Arches
**P** peach
   pear
**C** Canyonlands
   cherry

## VERMONT SUPPLY THE VOWEL

## VIRGINIA NAME THE PRESIDENT

1. s**W**amp
2. **A**ppomatox
3. pre**S**ident
4. Was**H**ington
5. Mad**I**son
6. Mo**N**roe
7. Arlin**G**ton
8. S**T**ratford Hall
9. Harris**O**n
10. Domi**N**ion

## VIRGINIA SCRAMBLED WORDS

1. Norfolk
2. Jefferson
3. eight
4. beef cattle
5. hams
6. soybeans
7. peanuts
8. Potomac

From *States of Wonder* published by GoodYearBooks. Copyright © 1992 Jeanne Cheyney and Arnold Cheyney.

## WASHINGTON CROSSWORD PUZZLE

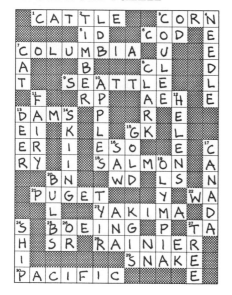

## WEST VIRGINIA CROSSWORD PUZZLE

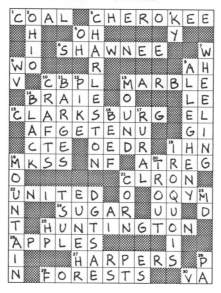

## WISCONSIN NUMBER CODE

1. America's Dairyland
2. Cave of the Mounds, with colorful stone formations
3. Apostle Islands: catch trout and salmon
4. House on the Rock: The rock is 450 feet high
5. gathering of waters, wild rice country, homeland
6. (1820) Some lead miners lived in caves dug out of the hillsides, like burrowing badgers.

## WYOMING CROSSWORD PUZZLE

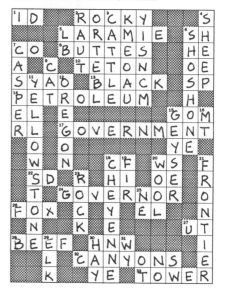

## WASHINGTON CROSSING OVER

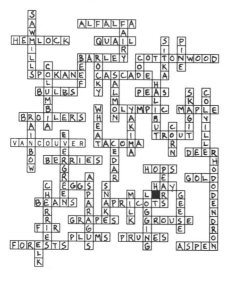

## WEST VIRGINIA RIVER AND CREEK PAIRS

| | |
|---|---|
| Big Sandy | Mill |
| Birch | Mud |
| Bluestone | New |
| Cheat | Ohio |
| Elk | Opequon |
| Gauley | Patterson |
| Greenbrier | Pocatalico |
| Guyandotte | Potomac |
| Kanawha | Tug Fork |
| Lost | Tygart Valley |
| Meadow | West Fork |

Shenandoah

## WISCONSIN CROSSWORD PUZZLE

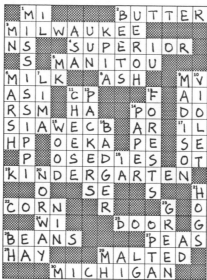

## WYOMING WORD SEARCHING

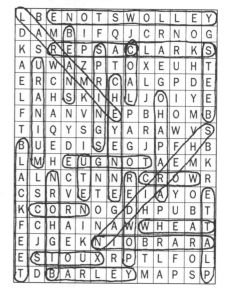